CANOE CAMPING

CANOE CAMPING

BY MARK SCRIVER

 THE HELICONIA PRESS

Published by

 THE **HELICONIA PRESS**

1576 Beachburg Road
Beachburg, Ontario
K0J 1C0
www.helipress.com

This book was printed in Canada by Custom Printers, Renfrew, Ontario.

First Edition

ISBN # 1-896980-22-8

Written by: Mark Scriver
Photography by: Jock Bradley, except as noted.
Illustrations by: Paul Mason
Cover design: Ken Whiting
Interior design: Robyn Hader
Editor: Rebecca Sandiford

About Safety

Canoeing and Camping are both
activities with inherent risks, and this
book is designed as a general guide, not
a substitute for experience. The publisher
and the author do not take responsibility
for the use of any of the materials or
methods described in this book. By
following any of the procedures described
within, you do so at your own risk.

Library and Archives Canada Cataloguing in Publication

Scriver, Mark

     Canoe camping / by Mark Scriver ; photographer, Jock Bradley ;
     illustrations, Paul Mason ; editor, Rebecca Sandiford

ISBN 1-896980-22-8

     1. Canoe camping. I. Mason, Paul (Paul D.) II. Bradley, Jock, 1961-
     III. Sandiford, Rebecca, 1973- IV. Title.

GV790.S37 2006   797.122   C2006-900843-4

TABLE OF CONTENTS

ACKNOWLEDGEMENTS

To my parents who sparked my interest in the outdoors, to my family who share my enthusiasm for canoe tripping, and to Black Feather Wilderness Adventures for the opportunities to meet hundreds of interesting folks and to adventure in the most amazing places on earth.

INTRODUCTION

Many of the most magical moments I've enjoyed in the outdoors have been while canoe camping. Canoe camping is a very simple pastime; yet there are so many opportunities for interesting and diverse experiences. Explore the possibilities and you'll be rewarded with your own magical moments.

Bill Mason said that canoe tripping is "living in the outdoors". As with life, there are a few wrong ways to do it, but there are an awful lot of different right ways. No matter which way you choose, you can be as comfortable, efficient, relaxed, active or lazy as you are in the rest of your life.

If you're new to canoe camping, this book will show you how simple and enjoyable it can be. You'll get a checklist of things you need to have, know and do to have a safe and pleasant experience. You'll learn to plan and carry out a trip efficiently and comfortably. If you're an experienced tripper, you already know that there are always new things to try as your skill and knowledge evolve. This book should provide you with some little tricks and ideas to simplify—or spice up—your next trip.

There is lots of room for creativity even in the simple tasks required by canoe camping—even more when you consider all the opportunities it affords you to pursue other passions such as hiking, cooking, whitewater, and photography. You'll

be encouraged to explore other activities that are complementary and will add to your adventure.

Canoe camping can't help but give you a greater appreciation of the outdoors. It puts you on intimate terms with the environment—from the large-scale, like a soaring cliff or a majestic waterfall—to the small-scale, like a frog on a lily pad, a turtle sunning itself on a log. This intimacy and familiarity can engender personal insights into how we fit into ecosystem and our role in its protection and conservation.

ABOUT THE AUTHOR

MARK SCRIVER

Canoeing and paddling have been a big part of Mark's life. He was introduced to canoe camping and outdoor activities with his family and in school. Soon after graduating, he began teaching canoeing and guiding trips for several camps in Ontario. Since then, Mark's paddling has taken him around the world. He has taught whitewater canoeing, sea kayaking and other paddling and outdoor skills, and has been leading commercial canoe trips for Black Feather Wilderness Adventures since 1983. Mark also co-authored *Thrill of the Paddle*—an instructional whitewater canoeing book—and is a former world champion of whitewater freestyle canoeing. Mark enjoys paddling with his family and exploring the interaction between his canoe and the water.

CHAPTER ONE

ROUTE PLANNING

CHOOSING A TRIP • CHOOSING A GROUP
PRE-TRIP PLANNING

CHOOSING A TRIP

Choosing an appropriate route is the first step towards a successful trip and is worth careful consideration. You don't have to go to remote or exotic areas to have a good time and some of the best trips can be to odd places, so be prepared to think outside the box.

Many national, state/provincial, and regional parks offer a range of possible routes for all levels. Official parks often have well-maintained portages and campsites, and detailed information about their routes is usually easier to find. Remember that many parks limit the number of people who can enter each day, and reservations may be required. For popular or more ecologically sensitive parks, you may even need to register or reserve months in advance.

While parks offer the most obvious options for canoe tripping, you'll also find good canoe routes on waterways with sections of privately owned land and cottages. Just make sure that there are adequate tracts of public land for campsites and stops during the day.

Guidebooks and word-of-mouth are among the best sources of ideas for routes. A good guidebook that provides detailed logistical information is almost a one-stop-shop for trip planners. Important information can include the location (and rating) of different campsites and routes, expected water levels, emergency takeout options and points of interest. 'Easy' and 'difficult' are relative terms however, so try to get some additional information before trusting a guide book completely. The Internet and the staff at your local canoe/kayak retailer can be great sources of information.

Whether or not a guidebook is available, maps will help you plan your trip, not to mention how important they are for navigation once on the water. I love maps and always feel like buying them is money well spent! Good maps show you the distances you'll travel, reveal elevations and landmarks, give you ideas for possible side hikes, and can (to some degree) indicate the difficulty of different routes. Government survey topographic maps are generally the best maps available for trip planning, but note that portages and rapids are not always accurately or consistently marked on them. Government topographic maps will usually show roads fairly accurately, which you can use as access points in case of emergency, or consider for takeout contingency plans in the event that you need to shorten a trip. Topographic and other maps are available from outdoor retailers, map stores, and government offices. Because it is difficult to keep every map in stock, sometimes the ones you need have to be ordered in, so be sure to get your maps well in advance of your trip.

Once you have gathered information about the different trip and route options you are willing to consider, there are a number of personal issues to take into consideration before you make your final decision.

GOALS AND OBJECTIVES

At the risk of sounding like a self-help book, it's very important to think about the goals and objectives of your trip before you get the maps and guidebooks and show up at the put-in. You might choose objectives such as: get some exercise, see some wildlife, avoid other people, or explore a certain area. All participants (especially kids) should be aware of the others' objectives, which should be reasonably compatible. It is easy to try to pack too much into a trip, like: get in shape, relax, unwind, lose 10 lbs, cook gourmet meals, see lots of wildlife, and learn to play the trumpet. Try to be realistic, even if the group objectives are to push fairly hard and cover a lot of distance.

BASIC ROUTE OPTIONS

The simplest of routes are an out-and-back sort: you go some distance from your put-in and turn back at roughly the midpoint of your trip. This type of route has the most flexibility and the easiest logistics. Even though you're retracing your route, the return trip can feel completely unique because you look in a different direction, and perhaps paddle an opposite shoreline.

If your route involves portaging, don't expect to be able to cover the same distance in a day. Although portaging can be a great part of any canoe trip, it is hard work and will undoubtedly slow your progress.

A one-way route allows you to see more terrain, but requires a shuttle by car, train or aircraft. Reliable locals or friends can sometimes be recruited to deliver you to the put-in or your vehicle to the take-out.

There are some canoe trip routes that loop, ending back at the starting point, and which offer the best of both worlds: straightforward logistics and new terrain for the majority of the route.

LENGTH OF TRIP

If you're new to canoe camping, an overnight or long weekend trip is a great length for getting your proverbial feet wet and honing some skills before embarking on a more ambitious trip. Some terrific places can be reached on simple overnight trips, and depending on how you plan it, weekend getaways can be relaxing breaks or refreshing adventures. On longer trips, it is easier to get immersed in "living in the outdoors" and settle into a relaxed rhythm. Remarkably little is different between the logistics of an overnight and a three week expedition, so don't be intimidated by the idea of planning a longer trip. Of course you'll need more food and books, but the equipment is the same, and it's great to have the time to venture into more remote areas. When I'm deciding how long a trip to do, I take the maximum time that I can get away with, add two days, and deal with the repercussions.

PACING AND DISTANCES

In planning your route, you'll want to make sure the distances you travel are compatible with the abilities and desires of your group members. A reasonable paddling pace with average canoes and average wind conditions on flat water is about 3 miles (or 5 km) per hour. Five or six hours of paddling will take about eight hours when you include lunch, snack and pee breaks, so most people will find 15 to 18 miles (25 to 30 km) a full day. If your route or plan involves portaging, hiking, exploring, photography or other activities, you should consider reducing the distance you plan to travel.

Don't measure distances in straight lines; it may be more interesting to follow the shoreline, and if the distance between campsites feels a bit short you can always take a detour and explore some bays. Whatever the distance you're planning on paddling, make sure that everyone is aware and capable of the daily paddling distances. Conversely, be careful not to underestimate how far you'll want to travel, even on a trip where one of the main goals is to relax. You might get bored from inactivity and miss some great scenery. As well, campsites don't always appear where you want them (or where they are supposed to be according to the map), and sometimes other groups will have already taken the campsite you intended to use. For these reasons, it's always best to have a rough idea of where you'll be camping, but keep an alternative or two in mind.

Photographer Jock Bradley, starts out on one of the many portages during a trip down Algonquin Park's Barron Canyon.

TIME OF YEAR

The time of year will have a big effect on your trip. In North America, the heaviest traffic on canoe routes usually occurs in July and August. Weather, water temperature and water levels will vary depending on the time of year. Average daily weather conditions are now available on the Internet for most places and a little research will help you to be prepared for the conditions you'll encounter. With the proper experience and equipment, a trip in the cooler temperatures of fall or spring can be very rewarding. You'll see fewer people and perhaps more wildlife, and can enjoy the spring blooms or fall colors. However, don't underestimate the danger of hypothermia. Wetsuits—or better yet drysuits—are recommended if there is any possibility of an unexpected dunk in cold water.

CHOOSING A GROUP

The most important factor in choosing a group is that everyone's goals and objectives as well as their skills and conditioning fit within the parameters of the route you're choosing. They don't have to be the same; one of the ways to improve your skills is to go with more experienced paddlers and you can broaden your horizons by going with people with different interests such as photography or birdwatching.

The group dynamic will be very different depending on the number of people in the group. With larger groups, cooking takes longer, the number of tent sites required reduces your choices of campsites and the group can get quite spread out on the water. However, there are lots of hands to help in the chores and more people to chat and interact with. With smaller groups there are fewer hands for the chores and or serious emergencies. Generally 12 is considered a recommended maximum group size. My favorite group size is eight.

Some parks have restrictions on group size. Environmental concerns and the size of the campsites will also impose limits. More people mean more tent sites, more firewood, more human waste, and more traffic on the land. Some campsites, such as gravel bars that get flooded each spring can sustain more traffic than a fragile, dry environment where disruption from a tent site can kill vegetation that requires decades to regenerate.

PRE-TRIP PLANNING

SAFETY

Let someone know your planned route and when you'll be returning so that if you're not back on time they can alert authorities. Give them the number of the park office or a local authority they should contact. You should have health and medical information, and a contact person for each member of the group. Depending on the remoteness of your trip, consider taking a cell phone if there is coverage, or a satellite phone or VHF radio for emergency communication.

RESEARCH

Because waterways and canoe routes were the highways of exploration for a few hundred years, they are rich in history. You'll find that historical landmarks and routes are the most interesting when you're standing right on them or camping beside them. By doing a little bit of research in advance you can make a trip much more rewarding.

Canoe camping can take you to magical and remote locations. Although this is one of the great joys of canoe trips, it means that you need to be prepared for emergency situations that could arise.

Reading up on official histories is not the only way to get a sense of a place. If you're lucky you'll encounter people who can tell you about their own personal experiences in an area. A friend of mine once guided a father and son on the Nahanni River. The father had been a trapper there in the 1920s. He was able to find the remains of his old winter cabin and relate details about the life he lived there to the rest of the group.

Canoe trips can be great opportunities to learn more about natural history as well. Geographical and geological features are more exposed in riverbeds and valleys. I've had geologists and gemologists on trips with me who were able to point out interesting landforms and rocks and explain how the local geography was formed. You'll also find the greatest biodiversity of flora and fauna near waterways, and may want to take wildlife or plant identification books along on the trip.

CHAPTER TWO

EQUIPMENT

**PADDLING GEAR • CAMP GEAR • KITCHEN EQUIPMENT
CLOTHING • SAFETY GEAR AND ACCESSORIES
OTHER PERSONAL STUFF • EQUIPMENT LISTS**

In this chapter, we take a quick look at different pieces of equipment for canoe camping—some of which are essential and some of which are luxuries that you may want to consider acquiring. At the end of this chapter, you'll find a couple of equipment lists that are designed to help you plan your trip. As you gain experience, you'll refine your own equipment list, learn the idiosyncrasies of your gear and appreciate the qualities of a finely crafted tool.

PADDLING GEAR

CANOE

To accommodate storage or budget constraints, most people will borrow or rent canoes for the first few years. This approach also gives you the opportunity to try different kinds of canoes before you make the big purchase. As you gain paddling experience, you'll start noticing more about how different canoes interact with the water, and what features you like and dislike.

When choosing a canoe, your paddling style and the type of trips you prefer will determine your priorities for canoe performance. The length and width of the canoe will then be your first and most important consideration. Longer canoes (typically in the 17 to 18.5 foot range) will generally be faster, have more carrying capacity and living space. Shorter (typically about 16 feet and under) canoes will be more maneuverable. Wide canoes are more stable and have larger carrying capacities, but they are slower moving through the water than narrow canoes.

You'll also need to consider such things as the rocker of a canoe. Rocker is the curvature of a canoe's hull from bow to stern. The more rocker a canoe has, the more maneuverable it will be, but the less easily it will keep a straight line. Rocker comes in handy on constricted waterways or in current, when maneuverability is a real asset.

The material a canoe is made from will determine its weight, durability and cost. Composite materials include carbon, Kevlar, and fiberglass. While all composite canoes are subject to more damage from heavy collisions than other canoes, they will last for years if treated carefully. Canoes made from carbon or Kevlar are considerably lighter than all other canoes, with light and ultra-light models of different lengths weighing anywhere between 40 and 65 lbs. This makes them great for portaging or for people who have trouble carrying heavy loads, but they are also much more expensive. Composite canoes available in fiberglass can vary greatly in price, weight and quality. Royalex canoes are about the same price and weight (usually anywhere between 60 and 85 lbs) as the average fiberglass canoe, but are much more durable and a good option for most people looking for a mid-range canoe. Polyethylene canoes are the

least expensive and quite durable, but they are by far the heaviest of canoes.

Finally, hand-made wooden canoes, including the classic cedar canvas canoe, are favored by some because they are beautiful, feel great in the water, and have the appeal of being traditional. Drawbacks include their weight for portaging, and their durability. Since they require more caution in their use and maintenance than synthetic boats, they are not recommended for beginner canoe campers.

Canoe Outfitting

There are a few little pieces of outfitting that can help make your canoe a bit easier to handle. I recommend attaching a thin but strong 12 or 15 foot (4 or 5 meter) rope to the bow of your canoe (also called a "painter") so you can tie it up at a moment's notice.

If you find yourself heading out in rough conditions, tie a 15 foot (5 meter) length of rope to the canoe's yoke, then thread it through all the packs and tie the end to the last item. If the canoe capsizes, everything will stay attached but will be able to drift far enough away from the canoe that a rescue and righting the boat will be easier.

All boats should have a bailer. You can also use a 1 gallon (4-liter) plastic jug with the bottom cut out as bailer. Clip it to the canoe with a carabiner so that it's easily accessible and won't get lost.

Some other standard things to outfit your canoe with are:
- a throw-bag with at least 50 feet (16 meters) of rope
- a whistle
- an extra paddle
- a waterproof flashlight if you're going to be on the water after dusk

PERSONAL FLOTATION DEVICE

Your life jacket or 'personal flotation device' (PFD) is the most important piece of safety equipment, so make sure that you take the time to find one that is approved by the Coast Guard and that is comfortable enough that you won't ever feel the need to take it off while on the water.

There are many different styles of PFDs, because people come in all shapes and sizes. Paddling-specific models are by far the best because they deliver the flotation you need in low-profile designs that don't restrict movement. A properly-fitting PFD should be very snug, but still comfortable when cinched down. Although not necessary, pockets on a PFD can be useful for carrying sunscreen, a knife, gloves, or a snack.

Paddling-specific PFDs deliver the flotation you need in low-profile designs that don't restrict movement.

PADDLE

The paddle is your personal connection between the canoe and the water. Paddles come in a wide variety of shapes, sizes and prices, and so choosing a paddle can be a daunting task. Put your mind at ease with the knowledge that for any short and reasonably mellow canoe trip, just about any paddle that will propel your canoe and stand up to the rigors of the trip is perfectly adequate. For longer and more involved trips, having a paddle suited specifically to the job is more important for comfort, efficiency and enjoyment. Let's take a quick look at the ideas behind different design features.

Canoe paddles come in a wide variety of shapes and sizes to accommodate paddlers of different sizes and to suit different purposes.

If you're going to find yourself in any type of moving or shallow water, a shorter, wider blade is preferable, while a longer and narrower blade works best in deep, flat water. Canoe paddles can have either a straight shaft or a bent shaft. The bent shaft doesn't just look funky and cost more—it's actually designed to make your forward stroke more comfortable and efficient. Its value is a topic of great debate and not something that we're going to get into, but it is worth trying one out to see if it feels better for you.

Choosing a paddle of a proper size will also help make your paddling more efficient. If you're using a straight-shaft paddle, your top hand should be around your chin when paddling. To determine an appropriate shaft length, sit down and measure from your seat to your chin, then add 6 inches to cover the distance from your seat to the water. If you can't or don't want to measure the shaft length this way, you can use the following as a general guideline: paddlers under 5'8" will use a paddle 56" or shorter; paddlers between 5'8" and 6' will use a paddle between 57 and 60"; and paddlers over 6' will use a paddle over 60" long. Note that the blades are shorter on bent-shaft paddles so if you choose one, you will usually go for a paddle that has a shorter overall length. For example, someone who is 5'10" might use a bent-shaft paddle that is 54".

Even with all these guidelines, the most important consideration when choosing a

A good rain fly will cover any part of a tent that is not waterproofed, will provide ventilation, and have a good size vestibule.

paddle is to use one that feels and looks good to you. It has been anecdotally proven that paddling power and efficiency magically increase when you love your paddle.

The last thing to note about paddles is that every boat should have a spare one in case a paddler's primary paddle is damaged or lost. The spare paddle does not have to be as good as your main paddle, but should be good enough that you could still comfortably use it for a whole trip.

CAMP GEAR

TENT

The tent will be your home away from home, so choose it wisely. On warm summer trips, with few bugs, in protected areas, any old tent will do. On trips with constant rain, headwinds and cold weather, a secure refuge will provide a big psychological boost to your sense of well-being. There is an incredible number of tents out there to choose from with a wide range of features too great to discuss here. The folks at your local outdoor specialty shop can help you pick one that meets your needs and your budget, but before you go, here are some things to consider.

For driving rains you'll want a good rain fly that covers any part of the tent that is not waterproofed. In windy conditions, you'll want a tent that is stable, and this is determined by the number and configuration of the poles. Ventilation is critical to regulate heat and moisture in warm and cold conditions. A feature you will quickly appreciate is a vestibule, which is outside of the screened-in sleeping area but still sheltered. It is a great place to leave your day pack, shoes and wet clothing. The tent's weight, bulkiness, and ease of set up and take down are only moderate concerns on canoe trips; however, you should consider these things if you plan to also use the tent for backpacking trips.

As a final note, I would recommend that you spend the extra money for a good, roomy, well-designed tent. Not only will it last longer, but I can guarantee that over its lifetime you'll see enough nasty weather to make it well worth the additional cost.

Packing Your Tent

Although an empty nylon tent dries quickly when it is set up, it is best to pack the tent dry instead of damp. Of course, this isn't always possible, so you'll want to have a small waterproof stuff sack for the rain fly. If you're packing your tent with other gear, you'll also want to put the tent in a dry bag to keep the other stuff dry. I like to pack the tent in a dry bag, and then put the dry bag in a pack or barrel.

SLEEPING BAG AND SLEEPING PAD

Unless you want to spend a miserable night in the outdoors, make sure that you take a sleeping bag rated for the temperatures that you'll be experiencing. If it is a little cooler

A compressor sack helps reduce the bulkiness of a sleeping bag when packed.

than you expected at night you can gain five degrees in rating by wearing socks, a layer of fleece and a toque.

In general, sleeping bags are insulated with either synthetic fill or down. The advantage of synthetic fill bags is that they still insulate when they are damp and they are less expensive. The downside is that they are heavier and bulkier than down-filled sleeping bags, although a compressor stuff sack will help reduce the size of any bag when packed.

When it comes to sleeping pads, all you need to know is that thicker is warmer and more comfortable. Seeing as size and weight are not big concerns when canoe camping, it is worth going for a full-length, thick, inflatable sleeping pad.

TARP

A large tarp, usually suspended between trees to form an open-air shelter, can make a huge difference when canoe camping and is well worth the investment. Although you can get away with using a tarp as small as 6' x 8', it's hard to have a tarp that's too big. A tarp 18' x 18' in size will comfortably host a group of up to 12, and once you've used

Camping-specific tarps are light, strong, have lots of reinforced attachment points to make them easy to pitch, and will stand up to almost any weather.

one this size, you'll probably continue to use it even with a much smaller group.

Once you've decided on a size, there are a number of types of tarps to choose from. Your typical industrial 'blue' tarp will do the trick in many cases, although they tend to have a very short lifespan. In fact, strong winds and rain can destroy them in no time because the grommets in the corners and around the edges can be easily ripped out. Camping-specific tarps are lighter, have reinforced corners and edges, and even have attachment points in the middle of the tarp to hold a pole. These tarps cost more but if they are pitched well, they can stand up to almost any weather that Mother Nature can hurl at you.

PACKS

For the more basic trips that don't involve challenging waters or portaging, and that are close enough to home that wet gear isn't a major concern, you can get away with very simple packing systems. Waterproofing might be as simple as stuffing your gear into strong plastic garbage bags. You might even just wrap all your gear bags in a tarp inside the canoe to keep water and rain from drenching your gear. There's nothing wrong with getting creative and using everyday household items for your canoe trip, but you need to understand that these methods do limit the types of trips that you can go on.

On longer or more remote trips, it is simply not safe to travel without proper packs because wet gear and lost food or equipment can present very serious problems. As you pack for longer or more remote trips, it can be helpful to imagine how you'd fare if your packs ended up floating in the lake or drenched in a downpour. If everything important is secured in waterproof packs or containers, you'd be just fine. This section describes the types of packs you can choose for safely packing your canoe camping gear.

Barrel Packs

The barrel pack is a 10 to 15 gallon (30 to 60 liter) plastic barrel that has a metal clamp and gasket that secures a plastic lid on top and creates a waterproof seal. Most outdoor stores sell them with a harness system that makes them easy to carry. The great thing about barrel packs is that they are easy to load, comfortable to carry, and they last forever. This makes them ideal packs for personal equipment, although they are particularly useful for carrying food. They protect the contents from bruising and are also fairly smell-proof and secure against critters. I have even seen a barrel that a curious black bear unsuccessfully tried to investigate. There were claw and teeth marks all over the barrel but no perforations.

Dry Bags

Dry bags are reliable and functional options for waterproofing equipment and they come in a huge variety of sizes and styles. You can get them small enough for carrying a snack, or you can get them large enough to carry all your personal gear. Some even have extra features such as a clear panels that allow you to see what's inside, a purge valve to remove excess air, or a backpack harness system to make carrying them easy. Dry bags can also be relatively inexpensive, and last a long time if treated properly.

The key to keeping a dry bag waterproof is to close it correctly. If you are using a roll-down model, make sure that you flatten the opening, that you fold it over a number of times, and that you secure the ends.

Dry bags with backpack harness systems are much easier to carry.

Canoe Packs or Internal Frame Packs

A canoe pack is a large nylon or (traditionally) canvas pack that doesn't have a frame, but has shoulder straps and a capacity of 20 to 30 gallons (80 to 120 liters). They are the largest of your carrying options and the easiest to pack, but they are not waterproof. This means that you'll need to use several smaller dry bags inside the canoe pack. To make carrying them easier, canoe packs sometimes have a tumpline in addition to shoulder straps. The tumpline goes across your forehead and takes some of the weight off the shoulder straps. When the tumpline is adjusted properly it is quite comfortable but doesn't allow you to move with your head and neck.

An internal frame pack is very similar to the canoe pack, but it is usually slightly smaller and has a more comfortable harness system with a hip belt. Internal frame packs are the most comfortable system for carrying heavy loads over long distances.

Wanigan

For the kitchen equipment, you might consider using a wanigan. A wanigan is a large box made from thin plywood or plastic and is used to carry the pots and kitchen equipment. Some have a gasket to help keep the contents dry although not all of them do.

The advantage of the wanigan is that it makes it easy to organize the kitchen equipment and at camp it provides a nice flat area to sit on or play chess and checkers. The disadvantage is clear when you try to carry one. They are best carried using only

A tumpline is the best means for carrying a wanigan, and your PFD can provide welcomed padding for your back.

a tumpline attached close to, or at the top of the box and the loop should extend about 12 to 16 inches (30 to 40 cm) beyond the attachment points. When you are carrying it, lean forward and distribute the weight between your straight spine (via the tumpline) and your shoulders (with the box resting on your shoulder blades). Carrying a wanigan demands a certain psyche. This psyche ideally comes with a stocky body, no neck, and a hunger for punishment.

Day Pack

Day packs are great for keeping the stuff that you'll want throughout the day easily accessible—like raincoat, extra clothing layer, hat, sunscreen, first aid kit, water bottle, snack, sunglasses, or book. The day pack is also handy for side hikes. Of course, you'll want to keep the stuff inside your daypack dry, so either your daypack needs to be waterproof, or you'll need to use a dry bag inside of it.

OTHER CAMP GEAR

Lighter and Matches

These are essential items, so have a couple of extras in case they run out, are lost, or get wet. Matches, even waterproof ones, should be kept in a waterproof container. Do not rely on the waterproof-ness of waterproof matches.

Saw

A collapsible camp saw with a 12-15 inch (30-40 cm) blade is very useful for cutting firewood and for cutting poles to set up your tarp.

KITCHEN EQUIPMENT

Most of the kitchen equipment on our equipment list is self-explanatory and easily plundered from your kitchen at home. You can substitute your preferences or what is available, but here are a few explanations about some of the items.

POTS

Aluminum pots were common for camping until they were linked with Alzheimer's disease, so look for stainless steel or Teflon-coated pans. It is nice to have a large, 2 gallon (8 liter) pot for cooking or heating water, and then depending on the complexity of your menu and the size of your group, another three to five pots with lids that nest inside. A wok is versatile and great for frying, cooking sauces, or entire meals for up to six people. It can also be used as a washing basin for dishes.

If you are cooking over fire, the pots will get black—and it will be a losing battle to avoid it. Keep the kitchen equipment in stuff sacks, and use pliers or leather gloves to handle them to prevent the spread of soot. The pots won't get sooty if you use cook stoves. I have two pot sets, and if I'm on a trip on which I'm using stoves exclusively, I take the set that never gets used on a fire.

For information about stoves, see the section about "Cook Stoves" in Chapter 4.

OTHER EQUIPMENT

One or two stainless steel mixing bowls are great for serving salad, mixing batter, or as a lid for the wok, and they'll pack easily with the wok.

Cooking with a firebox is efficient and environmentally friendly.

There are different options for making coffee but I prefer a tall 1 gallon (4 liter) pot with a handle so it can be swished around to settle the grounds. Others use a camping bodum, percolator, or paper filters.

There are lots of options for plates, bowls and cups but this works for me: for each person, skip the bowl and use a deep plate made out of a polycarbonate thermoplastic (like Lexan), a good-sized insulated mug, and a stackable thermoplastic cup. The second cup is handy for soup or a second drink, as well as measuring ingredients when cooking. A couple of extra Lexan plates are handy when chopping vegetables or grating cheese.

I keep the eating and kitchen utensils in a nylon apron with different pockets to keep them organized and handy. Included in the kitchen utensils are a couple of large kitchen knives, one or two spatulas, a couple of large spoons for serving or mixing, a soup ladle, a whisk, a grater, a small strainer (for the dishwater), a can opener and channel-lock pliers that serve as a sturdy pot lifter.

Leather work gloves are another essential for handling hot pots or moving the firebox and packing up anything that is sooty.

A fuel bottle with a screw lid is more secure than the containers that the fuel comes in, so it's a good idea to decant it into a better bottle. There are several types of outdoor ovens that you can take that will help you add variety to your menu.

For information about water filters, washing and the toilet bag, see the section about "Staying Healthy and Comfortable" in Chapter 3.

Keeping your kitchen equipment organized is important. A nylon apron with different pockets offers a great solution for keeping your kitchen utensils organized.

CLOTHING

A good basic approach to choosing the clothing you'll use on a canoe trip is to have two complete sets of clothing for the worst possible conditions. Each set should consist of several layers of quick-drying garments that can be mixed and matched to accommodate different conditions. If one set gets completely wet on the water, it should still provide warmth until you can change into dry stuff at the campsite.

In hot, dry weather, use light fabrics and light colors to stay cool. In colder temperatures, the key to staying warm and comfortable is staying dry. A waterproof and breathable jacket and pants are ideal as an outer layer for both rain and windy, cold weather. If you do end up with wet clothes, it is tempting to stay in your extra set of dry clothes when you're back on the water the next day, but if there is a chance of getting wet again, it is best to get back into the wet stuff. The paddling will warm you up and eventually dry the clothes. Most importantly, you're sure to have a dry set of clothing for the night at camp or in case of an emergency. I remember a cold morning on the Dumoine River with a couple of inches of snow at a Black Feather staff training trip when we had to pour the hot dishwater into our neoprene booties to thaw them. We were glad that we did though, because we still had our dry booties for that next night in camp.

Choosing the right footwear for canoe camping trips is tricky as there are lots of options out there. In general, you'll want footwear for your time on the water, which you can expect to get wet, and dry footwear for your time around camp.

FOOTWEAR

Finding good footwear for canoe tripping is not a problem, but narrowing the choices can be difficult. Some of the variables are the temperatures you'll be encountering, the terrain where you'll be traveling and the space you have. In general, you'll want footwear for your time on the water, which you can expect to get wet, and dry footwear for your time around camp.

On the water, some good options include sandals, river shoes, and neoprene boots. Sandals are comfortable for warm weather and can be worn on the water or around camp. A pair of neoprene socks with your sandals is a good combination on cool days or in cold water. River shoes are like quick-drying sandals with the sturdy soles, toe protection and support of a hiking shoe. These are ideal for whitewater, portaging, cool weather, or for terrain where your feet need more support and protection than a sandal can provide. A pair of old running shoes will work fine as river shoes, but they will take longer to dry and will be heavy when they're wet. Neoprene booties will keep your feet warm in cold water, but most don't have very good support for walking on rocky ground, and they take a long time to dry, leaving your feet soggy.

Around camp, you'll want to wear dry wool or synthetic insulating socks in waterproof hiking boots or shoes, although rubber boots are the ultimate in defense against water.

OTHER CLOTHING

People who don't commonly wear hats or gloves often don't think to bring them along, but they can make a big difference when living in the outdoors. A ball cap will keep the sun off your nose and the rain from your eyes, while a wide brimmed hat will

Staying protected from the sun means using a hat, sunscreen, and sunglasses.

give you even more protection from both. In colder conditions, a synthetic or woolen toque can go a long way in keeping you warm on the water or in camp. Having a dry pair of gloves or mitts to wear around camp is also great protection from the cold at night. On longer trips in cool environments, I'll actually bring a second, neoprene pair of gloves or mitts, which I can wear while paddling.

SAFETY GEAR AND ACCESSORIES

FIRST AID KIT

Bringing a first aid kit on every trip is simple common sense, although it doesn't do much good if you don't know what's inside or how to use the contents. This is especially important if you take part in more involved multi-day trips, or find yourself acting as the leader of groups. In these cases, it's highly recommended that you take a wilderness first aid course. Nevertheless, even with lots of first aid training, it is a good idea to have a reference book to help you identify symptoms and treatments. You'll want to carry your first aid kit in a waterproof bag or container. Having the supplies divided up into zip-lock plastic bags inside a single dry bag works well. You can also use a Pelican case, or a Nalgene bottle with a wide opening to store the plastic bags of supplies.

REPAIR KIT

Equipment failure can be either an inconvenience or a big problem. For short trips, bring a good multi-use tool, like a Swiss Army knife or a Leatherman, as well as a needle and thread, duct tape (which has almost endless repair applications), and aqua seal. On extended trips, this list might grow to include specific repair kits for stoves, tents, or canoes.

COMMUNICATION DEVICES

Most canoe camping takes place in areas where if an emergency arises, you'll probably be able to paddle or walk to get help. When this isn't the case, having a means of communicating with the outside world will improve your margin of safety. It is important to understand that no matter how well they are supposed to work in the area you will be traveling to, you can never 100% rely on these devices.

Satellite Phones

In truly remote areas, satellite phones will be your only option for communicating. While they are becoming more and more common, they are still very costly to own and operate. Renting them can be a good choice. As well as the dreaded emergency call, they can be convenient to change or confirm pickup information, or to stay in touch with people from the outside world. If you're making non-essential calls, be sure to leave enough battery power that you could still make several emergency calls.

Cell Phones

Cell phones can be very useful, but you can't rely on them because you never know when you'll be out of range or when the battery may run out of power. Cell phones are also susceptible to failure from exposure to water.

SIGNALING DEVICES

Signaling devices are used to get attention, and are usually saved for emergencies.

Whistles

A whistle is one of the best ways to get someone's attention. Three short and powerful blasts are a standard signal of an emergency situation, while a single blast is used to just draw attention.

Mirrors, Flares, and Smoke

On remote canoeing trips, you will want to have some kind of signaling device that can catch the attention of a search and rescue team. Mirrors are used to reflect the light of the sun toward a rescue aircraft. Flares are like small fireworks that are launched into the sky and work best on overcast days or at night. Smoke canisters can be very effective during the day, but are useless at night.

NAVIGATION TOOLS

Navigation tools are pieces of equipment that help you establish where you are on the water and how to get to where you want to go. Basic navigation is something that we all do instinctively (some better than others), and in many cases you won't need any real tools. For example, if you're on an isolated lake, you'll know that by following

the shoreline one way or another, eventually you'll get back to where you started. Similarly, when paddling on a river, you'll know that if you paddled upstream to begin with, by heading downstream on that same side of the river you'll get back home. Although navigation tools aren't necessary in these cases, when you start dealing with more complicated environments they will be essential gear.

Guide Books

Many areas have detailed paddling guidebooks that share valuable information and that offer trip suggestions based on skill level and distance. If there's one available for the area where you're going, I would highly recommend picking it up.

Maps

Although any type of map is better than no map, proper topographic (often called "topo") maps will be your most useful tool for navigation. Topo maps are available for almost every area in the world from map or outdoor stores, or from government departments. Most parks have maps available for their area that have similar information on them.

A waterproof map case is the best means of carrying maps and it also allows you to confidently carry electronics such as GPS units.

Topographical maps are the best maps to have on canoe trips. They can be found for almost any area in the world and are available in several scales, with 1:50,000 and 1:250,000 being the most useful for canoe trips. A 1:50,000 scale map shows sufficient detail for navigating most waterways. For example, at this scale, an island that is 30 feet (10 meters) in diameter will be shown accurately, but it might not appear on a map with a larger scale like 1:250,000. On longer trips I usually take 1:250,000 scale maps so that I don't need to carry as many maps, but if there is an area where more accurate navigation is critical, I'll take along the 1:50,000 maps to pinpoint my location. These more detailed maps are extremely useful when paddling around many small islands or doing some side-trip hiking in mountainous areas.

To carry maps and protect them against the elements there are specifically designed map cases. I prefer truly waterproof cases like the AquaPac Whanganui to water-resistant, zip-lock style map cases. Truly waterproof cases last longer and are secure enough to trust your electronics such as a GPS in them as well.

For more information about how to use maps, see the section about "Navigation" in Chapter 3.

Compass

The magnetic compass is another key tool of navigation, although they're only useful if you know how to use them. A basic compass will help you orient your map and estimate your direction of travel, but get one that has a housing that spins, the degrees marked and a direction-of-travel arrow.

We'll take another look at compasses in the "Navigation" section of this book in Chapter 3.

The compass is a key tool for navigation, but they're only useful if you know how to use them.

GPS

Handheld GPS units are amazing pieces of technology that can tell you almost exactly where you are. The only problem with them is that they rely entirely on batteries, and like any other piece of electronic gear, are subject to failure in the field. For this reason, you don't want to be totally reliant on a GPS unit to the exclusion of other means of navigation (like the trusty old compass and map).

Watch

Believe it or not, the wristwatch is a useful piece of navigation equipment. Use it in combination with your maps to calculate your average speed. Later, you can use your average speed and the time to calculate your distance traveled.

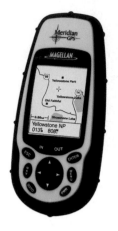

GPS units require practice to use properly.

OTHER PERSONAL STUFF

There are many pieces of gear that can make your canoe camping experience more enjoyable, and because canoes have so much carrying capacity, there are few reasons not to bring them along if you have them. The only reason not to bring that extra gear is if you have a number of portages to deal with, or if you'll be dealing with challenging paddling conditions. Here are some of the pieces of equipment that I consider important, and that I bring with me whenever possible.

Spare sunglasses - Having dealt with the discomfort of losing a pair of sunglasses at the beginning of a trip, I now carry a spare pair. Water reflects a lot of sunlight into your eyes and onto your face, and it's worth bringing some extra protection.

Camp chair - A simple foldout chair gives you back support and insulation for comfortable lounging on the ground.

Candle lantern - A candle lantern doesn't provide as much light as an LED headlamp but is great for reading in the tent or for general ambient light.

Toiletries - If you're carrying anything with your personal toiletries that a critter might consider smelly and interesting (including toothpaste, throat lozenges, deodorant, or

Most digital cameras are very compact and easy to bring along on canoe trips.

emergency chocolate), you should keep this away from the tent if you're concerned about bears, at least in a dry bag or even better in a barrel.

Binoculars - These greatly enhance wildlife watching, but can also be handy for navigation or checking potential campsites.

Logbook - As well as being a great means for capturing memories, the logbook can be a useful reference tool long after the trip took place.

EQUIPMENT LISTS

Here are two equipment lists that are designed to be starting points from which you can develop your own list. These lists have evolved over the years. I started off with very little in the way of gear. It is remarkable how comfortable and easily you can manage with very little equipment. If the lists looks daunting, look around your kitchen and garage, borrow or improvise, and see what you can do without (aside from a few critical items). I usually forget at least one critical item on each trip just to allow for creativity. I once forgot the dining cutlery for a 3-week trip. We all carved wooden spoons that some from that group still take on their trips to this day.

As your experience grows and your trips become more remote, you can modify your list to suit the trip and your personal preferences. To help with this, take time at the end of your trip and cross off things you took that were superfluous and add the items that you wished that you had.

BASIC TRIP EQUIPMENT LIST

On an Indian summer day between classes a friend suggested an overnight bike trip. About 10 minutes later we were cycling towards the Gatineau Hills with sleeping bags, matches, one spoon, a can of beans, a can of peaches and a half pound of cream cheese. Fortunately, the weather was warm and we had a memorable trip. For comfort and safety, I'd recommend a more extensive equipment list, but for a short summer trip without portages and navigation issues, you can get by and be safe with this equipment list of basic essentials. If you're just starting out, compare it to the more extensive list that follows to come up with your own equipment list.

Paddling Equipment

- ☐ Canoe
- ☐ Paddles (one per person and one spare per canoe)
- ☐ PFD with a whistle attached
- ☐ Bailer and 15 meters of floating rope per canoe

Personal Gear

- ☐ Canoe pack
- ☐ Tent
- ☐ Sleeping bag in waterproof bag
- ☐ Sleeping pad
- ☐ Headlamp or flashlight
- ☐ Spare lighter
- ☐ Personal toiletries in stuff sac
- ☐ Bug repellant
- ☐ Sunscreen

Clothing

- ☐ Two full sets of clothing (spare clothing in a waterproof bag)
- ☐ On water footwear
- ☐ Dry, camp footwear (with a plastic bag to keep dirt and dampness away from your other dry gear)
- ☐ Toque
- ☐ Sunglasses
- ☐ Hat
- ☐ A warm jacket (appropriate for the coolest temperatures you could expect)
- ☐ Rain jacket and pants

Group equipment

- ☐ Tarp in a stuff sack
- ☐ First Aid kit in dry bag
- ☐ Itinerary
- ☐ Menu
- ☐ Pen, pencil
- ☐ Repair kit: duct tape, multi-use tool, some extra rope or cord
- ☐ Maps in a sealable plastic bag or map case

Camp Gear

- ☐ Canoe Pack or barrel packs for food and kitchen equipment
- ☐ Pot set and fry pan (sizes based on menu)
- ☐ Cooking utensils
- ☐ Tableware (cups, bowls) and cutlery
- ☐ Lighter or matches
- ☐ Firebox and thick leather work gloves, or stove and fuel in fuel bottles
- ☐ 15 in folding saw
- ☐ Water filter or water treatment
- ☐ Large 1 to1.5 gallon (4 to 6 liter) jug for treated water
- ☐ Biodegradable hand soap and dish soap
- ☐ Bathroom kit

Food!

EXTENSIVE TRIP EQUIPMENT LIST

Here is quite an extensive equipment list of the things that I would take on a long trip with variable conditions. If you don't find it intimidating, you'll be on the Christmas card list of your local outdoor retailer. You'll rarely need to come up with all of the group stuff yourself though, and in many cases, you can rent or borrow items.

EXTENSIVE

Paddling Equipment

- [ ] Canoe

Included in each canoe:

- [ ] Bailer with carabiner
- [ ] 12-foot (4 meter) painter
- [ ] 15-foot (5 meter) rope to tie in packs
- [ ] 1 throw-bag
- [ ] Paddles (one per person and at least one spare per canoe)
- [ ] PFD with whistle attached
- [ ] Optional: river knife (attached to PFD and used in emergencies)

Personal Gear

- [ ] Tent in a dry bag
- [ ] Waterproof stuff sack for tent fly
- [ ] 1 quart (1 liter) Nalgene water bottle
- [ ] Insulated stainless steel travel mug with lid
- [ ] Sleeping bag in compressor stuff sac
- [ ] Sleeping pad (example: Therm-a-Rest)
- [ ] Camp chair
- [ ] Personal toiletries in stuff sack
- [ ] Logbook with pen or pencil
- [ ] Book
- [ ] Candle lantern
- [ ] Headlamp
- [ ] Spare sunglasses
- [ ] Extra lighter
- [ ] Deck of cards
- [ ] Dice
- [ ] Hackey sack

- [ ] Sunscreen
- [ ] Lip balm sunscreen
- [ ] Fishing rod and gear
- [ ] Biodegradable soap, extra toothbrush, moisture cream
- [ ] Bug repellant
- [ ] Frisbee

Packed in a waterproof camera case:

- [ ] Camera and film with waterproof case
- [ ] Spare batteries for electronic devices (GPS, camera)
- [ ] Binoculars
- [ ] Mini tripod
- [ ] Sunglasses
- [ ] Multi-use tool (Swiss Army knife or Leatherman)
- [ ] Bear spray

Clothing

This includes the clothing that is being worn.

- [ ] Cotton t-shirt
- [ ] Short sleeve polyester top with collar
- [ ] Short sleeve polyester top (running top)
- [ ] Long sleeve polyester shirt with collar
- [ ] Long sleeve polyester shirt
- [ ] Fleece vest
- [ ] 2 expedition weight long sleeve fleece shirts
- [ ] 2 polyester pants
- [ ] 2 polyester surf shorts
- [ ] Fleece pants
- [ ] Long underwear
- [ ] Bug jacket or bug hat
- [ ] 2-3 pairs socks and underwear
- [ ] Light hiking shoes (in a plastic bag to keep dirt and dampness away from other dry gear)
- [ ] Sandals
- [ ] Water shoes with a good sole and toe protection
- [ ] Neoprene socks that will fit inside water shoes or sandals
- [ ] Optional: Comfortable rubber boots for cold temperatures
- [ ] Toque
- [ ] Gloves

Packed in a day pack and dry bag:

- [ ] Rain jacket and pants in a 7-10 gallon (30-35 liter) dry bag
- [ ] Soft shell fleece jacket
- [ ] Sun hat with brim
- [ ] Neoprene mitts or gloves
- [ ] Baseball cap

Group equipment

- [ ] First Aid kit in a dry bag (one per group)
- [ ] Maps
- [ ] Compass
- [ ] GPS
- [ ] Cracker flares and signal flares
- [ ] Optional – two way radios with waterproof cases
- [ ] Tarp in a stuff sack
- [ ] Satellite or cell phone with emergency phone numbers and waterproof case

Repair kit in a dry bag:

- [ ] Multi-bit screwdriver
- [ ] Adjustable crescent wrench
- [ ] Small vice grips
- [ ] Needle nosed pliers
- [ ] Spare seat bolts
- [ ] Short bolts with washers to attach straps
- [ ] Needle and thread
- [ ] Small file
- [ ] Sharpening stone
- [ ] Sandpaper
- [ ] Quick ties
- [ ] 4 mm cord
- [ ] Snare wire or fencing wire
- [ ] Stove repair kit
- [ ] Duct tape
- [ ] Fiber tape
- [ ] Electrical tape
- [ ] Aqua seal for holes in dry bags
- [ ] 5-minute epoxy
- [ ] Aluminum tube just slightly larger in diameter than tent poles
- [ ] Spare tent zipper sliders
- [ ] Spare buckles

Camp Gear

- [ ] Barrel packs for food
- [ ] Wannigan for pots and kitchen equipment
- [ ] Pot set of 3-5 nesting pots (depending on group size)
- [ ] Wok
- [ ] Coffee pot
- [ ] Stainless steel bowl
- [ ] Griddle
- [ ] Cutting board
- [ ] Cooking cutlery
- [ ] Eating cutlery
- [ ] Cutlery apron
- [ ] Plates
- [ ] Cups
- [ ] Bowls
- [ ] Nylon stuff sacks for pots, wok, griddle, oven and plates
- [ ] Two-piece Dutch oven
- [ ] All-leather work gloves
- [ ] Camp saw
- [ ] Firebox
- [ ] Stove and fuel in fuel bottles
- [ ] Water filter or filter bag
- [ ] Large 1 to 1.5 gallon (4 to 6 liter) jug for treated water
- [ ] 2 collapsible water basin for dishes
- [ ] Hand sanitizer
- [ ] Bathroom Kit

Food!

CHAPTER THREE

ON TRIP

THE TYPICAL DAY • WATER TRAVEL • AROUND CAMP
STAYING HEALTHY & COMFORTABLE • MANAGING WASTE
ENVIRONMENTAL IMPACT

Finally the magic moment arrives when your canoe trip begins. You can forget about the checklists and last minute chores. All you need to worry about for the next few days is eating, sleeping and traveling. Every trip will be unique with its own highlights, challenges and special moments. Here are a few ideas that will help things run smoothly and let you enjoy living in the outdoors.

THE TYPICAL DAY

There are not many things that have to happen on a trip, and of those things, there are many different ways to accomplish them. There are so many variables that it would be hard to describe a typical day because sometimes you need an extra cup of coffee, pancakes take longer to cook than porridge, the second coffee necessitates an extra pee stop, a secluded bay needs investigating, wildlife poses when you're about to stop for lunch, you fall asleep on the afternoon float break, and the river grew since the maps were made. Nonetheless, here is a hypothetical list of things that might occur on a typical day.

- Start the fire or stove and put the water on 7:45 AM
- Coffee ready at 8:00 AM
- Get fruit ready for grazing and cook breakfast
- Water on for dishes
- Serve breakfast
- Do dishes
- Burn a small amount of garbage or bag it to burn at supper
- Take down tents and pack personal equipment
- Get lunch and snacks organized
- Pack kitchen
- Fill up individual water bottles
- Stretch
- On the water at 10:00 AM
- Float and put on sunscreen
- Paddle an hour and a quarter
- 15 minute break on shore for pee and maybe a snack
- Confer on lunchtime, look at maps
- Paddle an hour and a quarter
- Find a lunch spot by 12:45 PM
- Refill individual water bottles
- Prepare and serve lunch

- Dishes from lunch: either just rinse and bag the knives and dishes, or coldwater wash
- Pack up food and reload canoes
- Take 10 or 15 minutes to relax
- Back on the water at 2:00 PM
- Paddle for an hour and a quarter
- 5 to 15 minute floating or shore break
- Paddle for another hour and a quarter
- Pick a campsite between 5:00 and 6:00 PM
- Decide on a kitchen area and unload canoes
- Put up tents and change from river gear
- Put up tarp or get it ready if weather is threatening
- Collect firewood
- Start the fire or stove and put the water on
- Set up kitchen
- Organize food
- Hors d'oeuvres and drinks
- Cook dinner
- Put water on for hot drinks and dishes if pots are available
- Serve dinner
- Cook dessert
- Wash dishes while waiting for dessert
- Serve dessert
- Wash dessert dishes
- Burn garbage while washing dishes
- Pack up dishes, close barrels, pots on barrels
- Secure food, packs and canoes for the night

WATER TRAVEL

STRETCHING

Athletes rely on stretching to keep their bodies functioning in top form while being very active on a sustained, daily basis. While the intensity of output may be different, canoe tripping is about being active for a sustained period and it is worth taking a pleasant 5 to 15 minutes to stretch, loosen up and chat. Stretching also serves as a reminder to be conscious of your technique and posture, which helps avoid injury.

PACKING THE CANOE

For simple trips that don't involve challenging paddling conditions or portages, and that are relatively short in time, there are some very simple rules to follow when packing a canoe. As canoe trips get longer and more involved, your packing technique becomes much more important—because not only will you have more stuff to fit into your boat, but you'll have to consider comfort and convenience.

Whatever type of canoe trip you're embarking on, you'll want to pack your equipment in a way that keeps the heaviest items as low as possible, that spreads the weight as evenly as possible from bow to stern and side to side, and that leaves each paddler with enough room to sit comfortably and shift around. You'll also want to keep a day pack easily accessible, in which you can carry the things that you may want to get at throughout the day. For example, I'll keep such things as my camera, snacks, maps, knife, hat, sunscreen and sunglasses in my daypack. If the day looks like it could get damp and cold, I'll throw in a toque, gloves, and extra layer.

When packing a canoe for a longer trip, I usually try to keep the same gear in each boat for the duration of the trip. That way, when leaving the campsite or portaging, each canoe crew only has to worry about the equipment that belongs in their boat. Start with the personal packs of the two paddlers in that canoe, then divide the group equipment and food packs evenly. If there is any chance of capsize in difficult conditions, I like to have all the items tied in. To do so, tie a five meter rope to the

When packing a canoe, keep the heaviest items as low as possible and spread the weight out as evenly as you can from bow to stern and side to side.

yoke, then thread it through each of the packs in the canoe, and tie the end to the last item. The idea isn't to tie the packs in a way that will keep them in the boat in the case of a capsize. In fact, the idea is quite the opposite. There should be enough slack in the line so that if the canoe goes over, all the packs float free and don't impede the rescue of the canoe. The slack in the rope will also allow you to untie it from the yoke to free the packs, if required. If capsizing isn't a real concern, I'll only tie down the items that will sink (such as the firebox).

KEEPING THE GROUP SMILING

Whether you're taking the kids on a weekend trip, or heading out with a group of friends on a mini-adventure, there are a few simple ways that you can help keep everyone in your group happy and smiling.

The quickest road to discontent is through hunger and cold. If you can help those in your group avoid these two things, you're off to a great start. To stave off hunger, it's a great idea to keep plenty of snacks on hand and take regular breaks to enjoy them. Often there are interruptions that make a natural time to break, such as wildlife sightings or other points of interest. These are the times that I like to raft up with the other canoe(s) and to break out the water and snacks.

In some conditions, staying warm can be challenging and require constant monitoring. It is difficult to regain warmth once you've lost it—especially in wet and chilly weather. Staying hydrated is one of the best and most easily forgotten ways to keep your body warm. If you keep a toque and gloves in your daypack, along with an

If you want to keep everyone happy, make sure that your trip schedule offers the time to take breaks, stretch the legs, and enjoy a snack.

extra layer, it is easier to warm up if you feel a chill seeping in.

Although you don't need a precise itinerary for each day, you can make everyone's day more enjoyable by discussing and communicating the general idea of how far you're going to go, where you're likely to stop for lunch and to camp, and the options available for activities along the way.

The pace at which your group paddles is also very important. A sure way to turn someone's mood upside down is to exceed the pace or distance they are comfortable with. It can also be frustrating to go at a slower pace than you wish, so look for a balance to keep everyone happy.

Breaks throughout the day are welcome diversions. Often, this will mean hitting dry land so that you can hop out and stretch your legs, although if you've packed your canoe well, you should be able to take a comfortable break in your canoe. There is nothing quite as relaxing as laying back and floating in a canoe. Loaded canoes are very stable and several times I have fallen asleep during a floating break. When you're resting, you can raft up which is more conducive to chatting and passing around snacks. With a tailwind, or a little current, you might even find that you make good progress during a floating break. Something to keep in mind when taking breaks is that in any group there will of course be faster and slower paddlers. If you're one of the faster paddlers, make sure that the rest of the group is ready to go before you take off. Since the slowest boat is nearly always the last to reach a rest stop, they often get the least time to rest.

TIP

Unless you're on a tight schedule, it is always worth stopping for photo opportunities, but remember that you can't expect everyone to be as excited about the photos as you are. Having your camera easily accessible will help you take photos quickly and avoid frustrating the other members of your group.

NAVIGATION

On most trips, a map is all that you need to navigate. If you know approximately where you are and you have a decent map, you can probably match up most landmarks that you see with their representation on the map to pinpoint your location. This is easier if you orient the map or turn the map so it lines up with the features you see. In some cases, it doesn't really matter if you don't know exactly where you are. If you're heading to a portage at the end of a long lake, knowing you'll be there in a few hours is likely accurate enough. But if the campsite you're heading to is behind of one of twenty islands, you might have to pay almost constant attention to all the indications you have.

A map, carried in a waterproof map case, is often all that you'll need to navigate.

Topo maps, (as recommended in the "Navigation Tools" section in Chapter 2), use symbols and colors to identify geographical features. Water is usually marked in blue, vegetated areas in green and areas with no trees in white. You'll also find indications of roads, foot trails, bridges, swamps, rapids, buildings and other notable landmarks. Use the legend to decipher the symbols. Topo maps also have contour lines that show the altitude above sea level at a specific interval, (indicated on the map legend). These contour lines can give you a good idea of what an area will look like. If there are many contour lines close together, you can expect a steep incline. For another example, a mountain would be indicated by a series of concentric circular shapes with the altitude number of the lines increasing as the circles get smaller.

Whatever type of map you use, make sure that you familiarize yourself with the scale it uses. At the beginning of the trip, start off by looking for noticeable landmarks (such as islands or points), and see how big they look on the map. Having this rough understanding of the scale will make it easier to judge distance, difficulty of the terrain, and time required as you travel, and help you make practical sense of the map.

Using a Compass

It's a good idea to carry a proper compass along with your map. A good compass has a housing that spins, the degrees marked and a direction-of-travel arrow. You can use a compass to help orient your map, determine what direction you are traveling in, and pinpoint your position.

The red end of the compass needle points north and you can use this to orient your map. (North is at, or near the top of, most maps.) This is useful if you want to walk through the bush in a straight line looking for a portage trail or lake and then be able to retrace your steps.

The compass is divided into 360 degrees. Zero degrees is North. In a clockwise direction, east is at 90 degrees, south is at 180 degrees, and west is at 270 degrees. The direction you are traveling is called your "heading", and is referred to by the angle between north and the direction you are going in. To determine the direction that you are traveling, spin the compass housing to line up the red needle with the north indicator on your compass housing and read the number closest to your direction of travel.

You can use the compass to more accurately pinpoint your location in a couple of ways and they are described in the following subsections. As you read about these methods, it would be useful to practice with a compass and a topographic map.

Taking a bearing from a map

Before you can take an accurate bearing, you need to understand some terminology, as well as the fact that grid north is not the same place as magnetic north. The grid lines on most maps point to grid north. The difference between grid north and magnetic north is called declination. Declination is zero (grid and magnetic north are the same) on the Agonic line, which runs north-south, passing through western Lake Superior and Florida. Declination increases the farther east or west you go from that line, and is usually indicated on a good topographical map.

Let's say you are on an island that you have correctly identified on your map. Your map shows a portage on the other side of the lake, but you can't see any indication of it on the shore. Line up the edge of your compass with the island and the portage you want to go to. Turn the compass housing so the north arrow in the housing lines up with grid north. Let's say that the compass bearing is 310 degrees. The portage is basically northwest of the island. Let's say you are in eastern North America where the declination is 9 degrees west. When you take a compass bearing from the map, (which is using grid north) to a compass bearing, (which uses magnetic north) add or subtract the declination indicated on your map. In this case, because the declination is west of grid north, you would add 9 degrees to the bearing you got from the map and set a bearing of 319 degrees to reach the portage. To set a bearing on the compass, line the red end of the compass needle up with the arrow inside the compass housing and follow the direction-of-travel arrow. Remember, for this same scenario in western North America, you would subtract the declination because the magnetic pole is east of grid north.

Triangulation

If you are not sure where you are, but you can see two landmarks that you can identify on the map, you can triangulate your position. Take a magnetic bearing to the first landmark. Convert it to a grid bearing by adjusting for the declination (subtracting the declination if you are in eastern North America, and adding the declination if you are in the west.) Line up the north arrow inside the housing and draw a line from the landmark on the map. Repeat this for the second landmark. Where the lines intersect is your location.

Navigating with a GPS

A GPS will do everything your compass will do and more. One of the many functions of a Global Positioning System or GPS is to triangulate your position using three or more satellites. This position or "way point" is expressed in latitude and longitude (degrees and minutes) or as a grid reference. Your topographic map will have a scale with the latitude and longitude and likely a UTM (Universal Transverse Mercator) grid reference as well. The UTM system is easier to use than latitude and longitude and is the most universal grid reference system. There are many different grid systems

This DELL hand held computer, protected in a specialized waterproof case, was used as a GPS to plot waypoints on digitized topographical maps.

used around the world that you will see in the setup menu of your GPS. The manual of your GPS will explain this in more detail, or if you wish to use more than the basic functions of your GPS, take a course. There are two different types of GPS: "Number Crunchers" and "Mapping GPS". Number crunchers will record waypoints constantly to give you your velocity, altitude and a visual record of your track. You can also enter a waypoint that you want to travel to and it will give you the direction (as a magnetic or grid bearing) and distance to that waypoint. With a mapping GPS you can download topographic maps for the area that you are traveling in and save the step of getting grid references from the map. The mapping GPS displays your position on a map while the Number Cruncher displays your position as a co-ordinate. Even with these advanced features, and while a GPS is a useful and compact tool for navigation, your GPS should not replace topographic maps. Traditional maps provide much greater detail of information, and of course a GPS could always run out of power or malfunction.

> ## TIP
>
> Knowing how fast you travel is helpful for planning your days. Most groups generally travel between 2 and 4 miles per hour (or 4-6 km per hour) under ideal conditions. A group of relative beginners will cruise around 2 miles per hour, while a strong group will cruise closer to 3 miles per hour. Very fit paddlers who are consciously looking to cover distance may average closer to 4 miles per hour. Remember though that wind can have a dramatic impact on the distance you're able to cover.

PORTAGING

Portaging means carrying canoe and gear over land from one paddle-able waterway to another. Sometimes you'll need to portage around rapids, while at other times you'll need to portage from one lake to another. When you plan your trip, one of the most important decisions you'll need to make is whether or not your trip will include portages. If it does, you'll have to be more conscious about how you pack your gear and you'll have to make sure that everyone in your group is prepared to do some walking with loads on their back. Make no mistake—portaging is hard work, and as Bill Mason said, "anyone who says they enjoy portaging is either a fool or a liar." Still, you can derive real satisfaction from the accomplishment of a portage, and it can give you access to pristine inland areas that you would otherwise miss.

First of all, when planning and packing for your trip, you'll want to use fewer and bigger packs for your gear if you know that you will be portaging. You'll also want to make sure that the packs have shoulder straps, because carrying a loaded bag by hand is difficult and tiring. As a companion or alternative to shoulder straps, you can also use a tumpline. A tumpline is a strap that attaches to a pack (or canoe) and goes across your forehead.

Before you get anything on your back, a little organization can make the whole portaging process a lot more efficient. It is easiest for the crew of each canoe to look after their own canoe and gear. This limits the chance of gear being forgotten or lost in the shuffle. In most cases, it will take two or three trips to portage all your gear. If you're unsure of the way a portage trail goes, it's best to do your first trip with the easiest load so that if you make a wrong turn, recovering is easier. For this same reason, unless the path is very obvious, I don't recommend leading the way with a canoe on your shoulders. Your visibility is greatly reduced when carrying a canoe and you can easily go in the wrong direction on an unfamiliar path.

The canoe is usually the most difficult item to carry, although many people prefer carrying it to a pack. Although there is great truth to the saying that 'many hands make light work,' when it comes to carrying a canoe it can be easier for one person to carry it than two. The biggest challenge is usually getting it up there. Let's start by looking at a two-person, or tandem carry.

For a tandem carry, the idea is to lift the canoe over head and place it upside down with fronts of the seats resting on your shoulders and with both people facing the bow.

If your trip involves portaging, the trick is to use fewer and bigger packs for your gear.

With one person at the front of the stern seat and one person at the front of the bow seat on the same side of the canoe, you'll both grab the closest gunwale, then lift the canoe off the ground and rest it on your thighs. With the hand closest to the bow, reach across and grab the far gunwale about six inches ahead of the seat with fingers on the outside of the canoe and your thumb on the inside. Put your other arm under the canoe and cradle the hull. Using your hips and your arms, you'll simultaneously thrust the canoe upside down and into the air, turn your bodies 90-degrees towards the bow and set the seat down gently on your back. The edge of the seat should rest right on your 7th cervical vertebrae, (that boney bump that possibly evolved specifically for this purpose).

To carry a canoe solo, you'll need a yoke positioned in the center of the canoe, which will rest on your shoulders. There are a few ways of getting the canoe up there. You can lift the canoe with the two person technique and then one of you can shuffle your way towards the center of the canoe until the yoke is on your shoulders. To raise the canoe solo, position yourself in front of the yoke and follow the same steps for lifting the canoe as described above for the tandem carry. If you're having difficulty lifting the canoe using this method, you can lift the bow end and leave the stern end on the ground. You can then slide yourself backward towards the center of the boat. This method is slightly awkward, because the canoe will be balancing on the point of the stern deck. You can also damage or scratch a fragile deck doing this, but it might be your only choice. With the yoke resting on your shoulders, you can help balance

Grab the closest gunwale at the center and lift the canoe off the ground and onto your thighs.

With the hand closest to the bow, reach across and grab the far gunwale with your thumb on the inside.

Cradling the hull with your other arm, use your hips and arms to thrust the canoe into the air and upside down.

Let the yoke down gently on your shoulders.

the canoe by holding on to the gunwales in front of you. Some yokes have padding to make the carry more comfortable.

To take the canoe down, you'll simply reverse the steps we just looked at, whether you're carrying the canoe solo or tandem. Start by cradling the canoe with one arm while the other hand holds onto the gunwale. In a quick movement push the canoe up and off your shoulders, turn towards your cradling arm and let the canoe come to rest on your knees and thighs as gently as possible. You'll then move both hands to the near gunwale and lower the canoe to the ground.

Clearly, the toughest part about portaging a canoe is getting the canoe up and down from your shoulders. To take a rest in the middle of a portage without having to go through the whole process an extra time, use a tree with a forked trunk where you can rest one end of the canoe securely. You can then let the other end down to the ground and step out from underneath the boat for a stretch and a break.

To simplify getting a canoe on your shoulders for a solo carry, have a friend lift one end up into the air. You can then easily step into position under the yoke.

AROUND CAMP

CHOOSING A CAMPSITE

If you have a good guidebook or a trip report from a previous trip, you'll likely have a predetermined idea of where you'll be camping. On some routes campsites are plentiful but on others they are few and far between. You'll be spending a fair bit of time at the campsite, so it is worth choosing something that is as close to perfect as you can find, especially if you have lots of daylight. Although everyone has a different idea of the perfect campsite, some of the most common elements include good tent sites, pretty views, interesting areas to explore and good fishing. You may also want shelter from sun, wind, or lightning, an easy place to put up a tarp, or a windy spot to keep away the bugs. Some people like camping on sand. I'll admit that lying on the beach can be comfy, but I avoid sand when I can because it gets in food, zippers and everything else. I prefer smooth rocky areas. My favorite type of campsite is one that features flat stones on a large gravel bar. This kind of site offers plenty of tent space for everyone to spread out, and a good area for playing Frisbee.

Something you may or may not have to consider is the potential for changing water levels when camped close to shore. While camped on the Nahanni River, I rolled off my Therm-a-Rest at 5 A.M. one morning to find the tent bottom was like a waterbed. It had rained quite a bit the previous couple of days and the river level had risen over two feet (half a meter) in a very short period of time. Luckily my tent was the lowest and closest to the water. By the time I had woken the rest of the group and we had packed up, the river was running through our kitchen area. We would have lost at least a couple of pots if I had woken any later. Since then, I make a point of putting my tent lower than the kitchen when camped on a gravel bar with any chance of rising water.

PITCHING A TENT

After choosing the perfect campsite and unloading the boats, the nesting instinct takes over. When it comes to choosing a site, dry and level are the priorities, although you'll also want to make sure that you're far away from any fires. If there is no level ground, orient the tent so that your head will be on the high end while sleeping. Low points in the ground can often look inviting, but they can pool water if it rains.

Tents come in many shapes and sizes so make sure you're familiar with the setup of your tent before the first night of the trip. Many tents will not have waterproof flooring and need a ground sheet. If you put the ground sheet under the tent, make sure it doesn't extend beyond the tent as it will simply gather and pool water if it rains. You may want to lay the ground sheet inside the tent for this reason. You'll also want

Everyone has a different idea of the perfect campsite. Some people like camping on the sand, while others find sand to be a nuisance.

to make sure the fly is staked out and tight enough that it doesn't touch the tent.

If you're pitching your tent in sand, you can level out an area a bit by pulling sand from the higher ground down to fill the lower area. If the ground is too rocky to put in stakes or if you are expecting windy weather, tie cords to the stake loops, then tie the each cord to a good-sized rock or a stick that has rocks piled on it for extra reinforcement.

The tent can be a cozy bedroom and a relaxing place to hang out. If it's dark, a candle lantern will provide some ambient light, provide a bit of warmth, and remove some humidity. Remember though that any time you have a flame near a tent you need to be extremely careful. Although most tents are treated with a fire retardant, sleeping bags and clothing are not.

KITCHEN AREA

Although it's only natural to want to pitch your tent in the most beautiful location of the site, the majority of your time at camp is spent in the kitchen area and so it should take precedence. When choosing a kitchen area, you'll want to make sure you're satisfying as many aesthetical and functional factors as possible. These factors include: a good view, comfortable lounging, easy to tarp if the weather is inclement, close to water, and not too far from the tents.

Once you've staked out the kitchen area, and erected a tarp (if necessary), you'll

The bottom of an overturned canoe provides a flat raised surface
that is great for preparing food.

want to establish an area to set out and prepare the food. A flat rock shelf will work well for this or you can use the bottom of an overturned canoe. This is an advantage of flat bottomed canoes. By propping the upside-down canoe up with rocks or logs, or digging the ends down into a gravel or sand bar, you can quickly transform it into a spacious table.

However you set up your kitchen area, do your best to keep it as clean as possible. Not only is a clean kitchen more hygienic, but it will go a long way towards preventing unwanted visitors, like bears.

TARPOLOGY

In nasty weather your tent is your bedroom, but the tarp is the kitchen and living room so it's worth taking the time to set one up. If there's any possibility of rain when you get to your campsite, get your tarp up as soon as you've pitched your tent. With four or more people helping, it can be done very quickly. Some of my most content memories are of hanging out under the tarp with a coffee or bit of soup, watching the weather divide and go around us.

With a simple construction-style tarp, and ropes at each corner, you can attach the ropes from two of the corners higher and the other two lower to form a single pitched roof. To give your tarp a peaked roof, spread the tarp over a rope that is taught between two trees before securing the corners. This will give you more headroom and will collect less rainwater.

A good and simple tarp construction involves spreading a tarp over a rope that is taut between two trees and then securing each of the four corners.

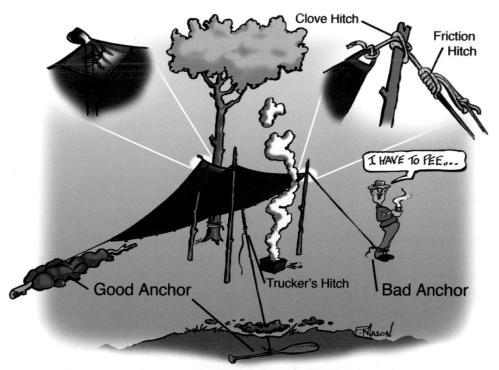

A camping tarp with a center pocket and reinforced corners offers the best combination of headroom, shelter, and stability in the wind.

For the best combination of headroom, shelter and stability in the wind, you'll need a camping tarp with a center pocket and reinforced corners. They're more expensive but will last longer and provide much better shelter. You'll need a 10 foot (3 meters) center pole which you can often find among driftwood. Start by tying the pole to the center pole pocket so it doesn't slide out an inopportune time. Attach two slightly shorter poles to the two corners where you want the open side of the shelter. Any old knot will do, but a clove hitch works well here. Next, anchor the ropes from all four corners. For the most stability and coverage, pull outward from the corners evenly and anchor the ropes at least 20 feet (7 meters) away for the front corners, and 12 feet (4 meters) away for the back corners. To finish off your shelter, you can place an overturned canoe at the back to keep firewood dry and to help deflect wind.

TIP

There are a number of ways to anchor a rope. It is easiest to anchor a rope around a tree, but if there isn't a proper tree you can use a large rock, several smaller rocks, or a paddle or stick that is held down by rocks. In sand or on a gravel bar you can even bury a paddle. It's good to be able to adjust the tension when you're raising the tarp so I use a friction hitch or a trucker's hitch. If the corners don't have strong reinforced attachment points or if they've ripped out, use a clove hitch or similar knot around the corner of the tarp in which you've wrapped a golf ball-sized stone.

CLOSING CAMP FOR THE NIGHT

When the evening is spent and you're ready for bed, there are few things that must be done beforehand. Most importantly, you need to make sure that the food and garbage is cleaned up and put away. Little critters are nearly always a concern, and a good reason for food to get packed away securely. If the area you're in has bigger critters to be concerned about (bears in particular), you have all the more reason to deal with your food properly. If bears live in the region you are visiting, you need to take some serious precautionary measures. The best way to keep bears out of your camp is to not tempt them with the smells of food. This means that dirty dishes should be cleaned and food and garbage should be packed in odor-proof containers such as barrels. You can even take the extra step of removing them from camp completely. If you're removing the food and garbage from your camp, the best way to prevent it from being pillaged is to hang it in a tree. Keep in mind that the forest's furry creatures are incredibly agile and

The best way to hang a food bag is to throw a rope over a thick, high tree branch, and then haul it up at least 10 feet (3 meters). It should also be 5 feet (1.5 meters) from the tree trunk and from the branch it is being hauled up to.

have probably already encountered similar challenges on numerous occasions. The best way to hang a food bag is to throw a rope over a thick, high tree branch, tie the bag up, and then haul it up at least 10 feet (3 meters). It should also be at least 5 feet (1.5 meters) from the tree trunk and from the branch it is being hauled up to.

On a final note, it's a good idea to save some tinder and firewood in a dry spot (such as under a canoe) to make starting a breakfast fire easier.

BREAKING CAMP

When it comes to establishing a game plan for the day, the night before is the time for negotiation. Without a plan established, mornings can quickly blend into afternoons with your group not yet having left camp. As a general rule for planning purposes, two hours is a reasonable amount of time from when the coffee is ready (nothing before that really counts), to getting on the water. Variables include the size of the group (smaller is quicker), how complicated breakfast is and how far you need to go that day. It is certainly possible to get on the water more quickly, but this allows you time to relax and enjoy a second cup of coffee, and to discuss the day's plan. The trick is to let everyone wake up at their own pace but be ready at about the same time. If you have some chronically slow risers, serving coffee or tea to them in the tent rarely elicits a negative response and will result in their need to pee.

STAYING HEALTHY & COMFORTABLE

The single best way to stay healthy on a canoe trip is to keep your hands clean. Hand washing won't always happen unless it is convenient, and there are a few easy ways of making it so. You can hang a water bag with a spout, or put out a folding water basin and a bar of soap. Hand sanitizer or individual wipes are convenient for lunch and snack times.

WATER TREATMENT

Although the water in many of the lakes and rivers on which you'll find yourself canoeing is safe to drink untreated, you can't ever be sure that there are not viruses, pathogenic bacteria and protozoa present. Even the most remote and clear streams can have them. Although some people will take the risk and drink untreated water on canoe trips, it's not a bad idea to treat all water before you drink it, and there are several methods you can use.

Boiling

Bringing water to a rolling boil is a great way of purifying water because it will reliably kill all viruses, pathogenic bacteria and protozoa. Just make sure the water comes to a full boil. Any of the water you use in cooking doesn't need to be treated if it is boiled at some point during cooking.

Chlorine

Chlorine treatment, in tablet or liquid form, is a quick and easy way to treat drinking water for a group, and is available at any outdoor specialty store. The only downside is the distinctive chlorine taste that results.

Miox Purifier

The Miox purifier combines non-iodized salt and a small amount of electricity from a battery to create an anti-oxidant and purify water as well as chlorine. It is a small, compact and self sufficient purifier.

Pumping water through a glass fiber or ceramic filter is the most common and practical method of purifying water.

Keeping your water treatment system easily accessible will take one hassle out of your day.

Filters

The most common and practical method of purifying that results in good tasting water is by pumping water through a glass fiber or ceramic filter. Depending on the model, you can expect to pump a gallon (4 liters) of water in 4 to 8 minutes. Glass fiber pumps are less expensive, but have a shorter lifespan (about 1,000 gallons.) Ceramic filters will pump up to 2,500 gallons before the filter needs to be replaced.

To prolong the life of your filter and prevent bacteria from growing on it in between trips, always rinse your filter in chlorine-treated water and allow it to dry completely.

WASHING YOUR BODY

One of the greatest things about canoe camping is that you can wear the same clothes for extended periods and it doesn't matter if you always look like you just got out of bed. There are, however, times when you'll want to get cleaned up. Some people also like to have a warm water wash and a shave every morning. If you are going to wash with soap, try to reduce the impact to the local environment and don't put soap in the water. You will usually have less impact by dumping soapy water in the active layer of soil. The best way of doing so, is to get wet in the lake, soap up on land, and then use a water basin or big pot to pour rinse water over yourself well away from shore. You can even warm the water up beforehand and have a nice warm rinse.

A more luxurious option is to use a solar shower—a 1 gallon (4-liter), collapsible container with a shower spout that you hang from a tree limb. The black container will absorb the energy of the sun to heat up the water. If you don't have time to wait for water to heat up, you can still get a warm shower by pouring heated water into the bag.

STAYING WARM

When it comes to enjoying a trip, there's nothing more important than being warm. The key to staying warm is protecting yourself from wind, wetness—and preventing yourself from cooling down in the first place. It is much harder to warm up once you've got a chill than to stay warm to begin with.

The clothes you wear will have the biggest bearing on your ability to stay warm. Make sure that you have a shell jacket within easy reach at all times that will protect you from wind that picks up, or a sudden rain. Just as importantly, you need to protect yourself from wetness that comes from sweating. There's no better way to chill yourself to the core than to have a wet layer against your skin for extended periods. Undershirts and pants made from synthetic materials that are designed to draw moisture away from the body are now widely available and very affordable. It's important to note that cotton is the all time worst material to use as an under layer. When cotton is wet, it will actually draw heat from your body. Of course, even with a good under layer, your best defense is to change into a completely dry layer as soon as you've stopped your

The key to staying warm is replacing any wet layer that is against your skin with a warm, dry layer.

heavy activity for the day.

Although your clothing system does have the biggest bearing on your warmth, there are a few other tricks that can make your camping experience toasty.

Although most people protect themselves from the air temperature very well, the cooling impact that the ground can have is often ignored. Your sleeping pad is the single biggest defense you have against the cold of the ground, and the thicker it is, the more insulation it will provide. A common mistake is using a three-quarter-length sleeping pad to save pack space. This leaves a quarter of your body in direct contact with the ground. A full-length sleeping pad will go a long way to keeping you warm throughout the night.

MANAGING WASTE

When camping, there is nothing more distasteful that encountering the waste of past campers. If you're going to camp, you need to properly manage your waste. There are three types of waste that we're going to look at: food waste, garbage, and human waste.

FOOD WASTE

If you are accurate with the menu quantities, you can minimize the food waste that you create, but you'll still have some to deal with. There are two good ways that you can deal with food waste: you can either treat it as regular garbage and pack it out, or you can burn it over a hot fire. If you don't have a hot enough fire or the time to completely burn it, put it in a plastic bag and save it for burning later. Something to note is that although burying your food waste is often the most convenient thing to do, it is not a good option because animals will smell it and dig it up. Animals that get used to scavenging human food usually become a real problem. Bears in particular—which naturally avoid humans—can become a nuisance or a danger if they become accustomed to human food, and under these circumstances often have to be destroyed by wildlife officials.

GARBAGE

There are two options for dealing with garbage—which includes both the garbage that you generate and the garbage that you will unfortunately find along your travels. You should burn the things that can be burned safely, and pack out everything else. If you've packed well for your trip, you really should have very little garbage to pack out.

HUMAN WASTE

There is nothing that will detract from your wilderness experience more than seeing used toilet paper. In some parks and in well traveled areas, outdoor pit toilets are provided. If they are available, be sure to use them. In some very high traffic areas that are ecologically sensitive, you may be required to pack out ALL your human waste. This isn't as challenging as it seems. All you need to do is put a toilet seat over a waterproof container. You then make your deposit and close it up. There are some great products on the market that do a good job of absorbing moisture and reducing smells.

In Algonquin Park, pit toilets are provided for campers.

Otherwise, you'll need to create your own, natural bathroom. If you're just urinating, in most cases you'll want to find a spot far from the shoreline or any trails. On high volume rivers or in dry areas that see a lot of traffic, it is sometimes preferred that campers pee directly in the water. If you're doing more than just peeing, you'll need to dig a small hole in an active layer of soil at least 40 feet (15 meters) from the shoreline for each trip you make. In this case, you'll want to carry a bathroom kit that is made up of a small trowel (for digging the hole), toilet paper kept in a plastic bag, some hand sanitizer, and a paper bag (lunch size) inside another plastic bag in which you'll place your used toilet paper. This paper bag will then be burned on the fire or packed out. Either way, you'll want to bring enough paper bags so that you can use a new one each day. The problem with burying toilet paper is that it doesn't decompose quickly and often is dug up and scattered by animals. This whole kit can easily and discreetly be held in a small dry bag and shared in a small group.

ENVIRONMENTAL IMPACT

It is impossible to have no impact on the environments that we pass through, but we can minimize that impact. As environmental awareness and education evolves, camping practices and the condition of outdoor recreation areas have actually improved despite heavier traffic, although it does remain an ongoing battle. Any contribution you make including letters and donations to environmental groups can make a difference to protecting the special places you enjoy.

CHAPTER FOUR

FOOD AND COOKING

COOK STOVES • COOKING WITH FIRE • BAKING • MENU
PACKING THE FOOD • BREAKFAST • LUNCH • SNACKING
DINNER • OTHER FOOD CONSIDERATIONS • DISHWASHING

Before even getting into the topic of camp cooking, it's important that you know that there is no right or wrong way to cook and eat on a canoe trip. Your meals can be as simple or complicated, dull or exotic, spicy or bland as you want them to be. For some, cooking will be an 'add water and stir' event and your local outdoor store will have a full selection of prepackaged meals to choose from. These meals have really improved over the years. Most of them are nutritious, the directions are simple and thorough, and the quantities are quite accurate.

For many people, cooking can be one of the most relaxing and enjoyable aspects of canoe camping. If you enjoy cooking, don't be intimidated by the thought of getting creative with your menu. You may lack some of the conveniences of a full kitchen, but there are a couple of key advantages to cooking in the outdoors. In particular, there is rarely a reason to rush the cooking process and so you can take your time and enjoy the task. There will also be lots of helping hands available. Those same people who mysteriously disappear while you're cooking at home can help with preparations, and more importantly, with cleaning the dishes afterwards. Another great advantage to camp cooking is that everything seems to taste better after a full day in the outdoors.

COOK STOVES

Cook stoves work very well in all conditions, can help minimize your impact on high-traffic routes or ecologically sensitive areas by leaving no fire scar or partially burned wood and by reducing the amount of firewood you use. They are also your only viable option in areas with insufficient wood. There are a number of types of cook stoves available and most are available as either a single or double burner unit. The single units are very lightweight and compact, while the double units are less expensive than getting two single stoves.

Liquid fuel stoves that use white gas are the hottest and most efficient stoves. The liquid fuel is pressurized with a pump and then is forced out a small adjustable hole as a vapor. Lighting these stoves is usually slightly more complicated than simply turning on the gas and striking a match, so make sure you have read the instructions and tested your stove before heading out on a trip.

Some stoves use Liquefied Petroleum Gas (LPG) in a canister that screws into the stove valve and lights easily. The canisters are not refillable but they can be recycled. Another type of stove uses methyl alcohol as fuel. These stoves are simple to use, but do not provide much heat and don't work as well in colder temperatures.

Regardless of what stove you are using, you can coax more heating power from your stove by sheltering it from wind. Windscreens and heat reflectors will also improve your stove's efficiency and are worth bringing along.

If you're using stoves exclusively for a group of up to six people, plan to use a little less than a quart (liter) of fuel per day. Even with this guideline, it's always a good idea to take an extra bottle—just in case.

Occasionally, stoves may need some field maintenance and there are specific repair kits for each brand of stove. Understanding how the stove works is the key to being able to fix or adjust them in the field, so take the time to read the user manual.

COOKING WITH FIRE

Cooking on a wood fire is a romantic art form and an encompassing experience. There's something very comforting about the warmth you feel while tending the fire and stirring the food, the mixed smell of burning wood and cooking food, and the stinging pain from smoke in your eyes.

If you're cooking over an open fire and using an established fire pit, make sure that there isn't any chance of the fire reaching a root or even the active layer of soil. The ideal fire pit is built on rock or sand. You can use rocks around the fire to shelter it from the wind and to support a grill 7 to 9 inches (15 to 25 centimeters) above the ground.

For environmental reasons and efficiency, I prefer to cook using a firebox rather than over an open fire. The firebox is a relatively lightweight, folding metal box that contains

Mark and Pete make a breakfast omelet on a firebox. The firebox is an efficient and environmentally friendly means of cooking on an open fire.

your fire and that has a sturdy grill on top. They come in various sizes, depending on the size of the cooking area that you want. The firebox also helps concentrate the heat from your fire, so it uses less wood and allows you to control the cooking temperature more accurately. With a pair of leather work gloves, you can also pick it up while it's burning and move it to a new location. One of the biggest benefits of the firebox is that it doesn't leave a fire scar in sensitive environments or at campsites where there isn't a safe and established fire pit. When it's time to break camp, you can use water to extinguish the ashes and to cool down the firebox before packing it away.

Whether you'll be cooking over an open fire or using an environmental firebox, before starting a fire you'll need to gather some firewood—and a good fire needs good wood. Cooking over a fire with poor quality or insufficient wood can be slow and frustrating. The biggest mistake is using wood that isn't dry enough. For environmental and practical reasons, do not cut any live trees. Dead and fallen branches, driftwood or entire dead saplings are preferred. Avoid cutting dead lower branches from trees close to the campsite or from anywhere that will have a visual impact. The best indication of suitable dryness is that the bark has fallen off. When it is found off the ground and has lost its bark, wood will dry quickly, even after a rainstorm, and it is also less likely to have rot. The heat for cooking will be easier to control if you use wood no thicker than 1 to 3 inches in diameter.

Starting a fire is a quintessential outdoor skill. It can teach you about science, patience and life itself. The key is to start small and gradually build the size of the fire. This refers to both the size of the fire and the size of the pieces of wood that you'll use. Start with toothpick-sized dry twigs in a bundle the size of your wrist and compact them as much as possible. These small twigs will catch fire quickly, but the whole bundle needs to stay lit and produce enough heat to ignite the larger sticks that you'll continue to place on top. At first you'll need to shelter your fire from the wind, but when the fire is established, a light breeze will feed the fire more oxygen and allow it to burn more strongly. If you're stuck with rain-soaked wood, you can use a knife to remove the damp outer wood and then shave off thin strips of dry wood to start the fire. You can also use paper or birch bark (only from deadfall) to help start the fire, but you still need enough small pieces of wood to sustain a flame long enough to ignite the larger sticks.

It is easiest to control the heat of a fire if you have a good bed of coals. The wood you add will then catch quickly and raise the heat, and if you have too much heat, you can remove a couple of sticks or rearrange the coals. With good wood and a bit of experience you can control the heat of a fire as well as you can with any stove or oven.

BAKING

Although you can have quite a bit of variety and happily survive without it, baking lets you add all sorts of goodies to your menu, such as fresh bread, muffins, cakes, lasagna, pizza, pot pies, and even roasts.

Baking requires even and consistent heat (around 350°F or 160°C). The trick to baking is to avoid overheating on the bottom and to get some heat from above. There is an element of trial and error to successful baking, but that's part of the fun. You might end up with a crispy bottom to your dish, but it's hard to completely ruin a meal. With a little practice, you can make meals as good as anything that comes out of your oven at home.

There are several types of ovens that you can use for baking in the outdoors, which we're now going to look at.

> **TIP**
>
> Sticking can be one of the biggest issues to overcome when cooking in camp ovens. To prevent sticking, warm the pan slightly to get rid of any moisture and then wipe a small bit of oil around the pan with a plastic bag.

DUTCH OVEN

The Dutch oven is a cast aluminum or iron pot that stands on legs and has thick walls that hold and spread heat very well. This is my favorite baking tool, despite the fact that it is a little heavy and bulky. To use a Dutch oven you'll want to have a thick pair of leather work gloves so that you can pick the oven up while it's cooking hot and move it around.

Although you can use a Dutch oven over a slow fire, you'll get the best results with the use of some charcoal briquettes that have been preheated over a fire, along with aluminum foil. You'll need about ten briquettes underneath the oven and eight on top. You'll then envelop the whole thing with tin foil (sides, top and bottom) to keep the heat in. If you don't have briquettes, you can use coals from a fire, but they don't give heat for as long.

*After placing hot briquettes under and on top of the Dutch oven,
Mark completely envelopes it with aluminum foil.*

OUTBACK OVEN

The outback oven is an effective, lightweight baking system. Although it doesn't work very well on an open fire, it is the best system for use with a camp stove. The outback oven consists of a Teflon-coated frying pan with a tight fitting lid; a heat-deflecting burner plate that prevents direct flame from hitting the stove and burning the bottom of your food; and a burn-resistant fabric hood that goes over the pan like a tea cozy and distributes the heat over the top of the pan. It also requires a stove with a separate fuel tank and burner so that the fuel tank doesn't lie under the hood where it can overheat. One of the nice things about the outback oven is that it has a heat indicator on the lid to help you keep a consistent cooking temperature. For best results, you can use a heat reflector around the system. An easy way to create a reflector that is the same diameter as the hood is to use two regular camp stove heat reflectors together.

BOX OVEN

The folding box oven by Coleman is designed to work on a two-burner stove, although it also works well on an open fire. As with all ovens, the trick to using the box oven is maintaining a consistent heat source. If you're cooking over a fire, this is most easily done with a good bed of coals instead of open flame.

The box oven is about 14 inches (35 cm) cubed and it folds to 2.5 inches (6 cm) thick. It comes with one rack that adjusts to three different levels and it has a temperature gauge that works well, but when used on the fire, the gauge becomes sooty and unreadable very quickly. After being exposed to extreme heat and water, you can expect the box oven to warp and rust, but this won't affect how it works.

REFLECTOR OVEN

The reflector oven sits beside the fire and draws heat in at the bottom and out over the top of the pan. The oven folds flat for transport, is about 12 x 12 x 20 inches (30 x 30 x 50 cm) when assembled, and has a single shelf that fits two pans side by side. Although some people swear by these ovens, I find cooking with a reflector oven to be challenging and prefer to use one of the ovens mentioned above.

POT OVEN (DOUBLE BOILER)

The pot oven works the same way that the box oven does, but it doesn't distribute heat as evenly. For best results, you're better off with a proper oven.

The pot oven can be used over an open fire or on a stove. To make a pot oven, put three stones inside a big pot, place a smaller pan (without a lid) on the stones, and then cover the two with a lid. The pan inside needs to be small enough to allow air to circulate so that it is easy to remove when the food is ready. For cakes or muffins that cook quickly, or don't require as much heat, you can put water in the bottom of the pot to prevent burning and to keep your food moist.

MENU

The menu is an important piece of the canoe camping puzzle. It is your master plan and you should take a couple of copies on your trip. In the planning stages, it determines how much food you'll bring, as well as how it will all be packed; but once on trip, don't feel handcuffed by your menu. I often switch meals around depending on cooking times, weather, or just on a whim. I've included a sample menu to give you some ideas of how I like to organize my trip. Whatever way you decide to set up your menu, there are a few things to keep in mind when planning it out.

First, your menu should make sense for the type of trip that you're embarking on. For a weekend trip with limited on-water travel, you'll probably have lots of time in camp to cook up a masterpiece using more fresh ingredients. On more involved canoe trips, you can expect to have much less energy for cooking and will want to plan for quick and hearty meals.

Having a reasonable variety in your meals is also important. It's hard to get excited about tuna for dinner when you just had it for lunch.

For cooking purposes, you need to make sure that you will be bringing enough pots and pans, and that you'll have enough fuel if you're relying on a stove.

Keep in mind how long perishable food will last. If it especially hot, you can't expect food to last long and so you may have to use up fresh vegetables earlier than you planned. You'll also want to minimize food that is bulky, overly heavy, or soft and easily crushed.

QUANTITIES

How much food to bring gets more complicated and more important to gauge accurately for longer trips. You don't want to find yourself carrying unnecessary food over long portages, but for safety reasons it is important that you bring a little extra food to accommodate an extra day or two of camping should your plans be affected by weather or other unforeseen factors. On a trip we did to the Arctic's Hood River, we were picked up two days late because of the weather but we got by quite happily on extra rice, soup and pancakes.

There's no simple answer when it comes to deciding on how much food to bring, as there are many factors affecting how much food people will eat. Some people just eat a lot more than others do. Appetites will also increase on days when you've been very active and in cold weather. When it's hot, people might eat less, but they'll use more drink crystals.

Breakfast

Day 1

Day 2

1 melon
2.5 c. Muesli
1 can evaporated milk

Eggs
12 eggs
.5kg bacon
1 onion
12 english muffins

Lunch

Day 1

12 bagels
500g cheddar cheese
500g salami
6 carrots

Day 2

12 pitas
3 cans tuna
2 celery stalks
250g cheddar cheese
100ml salad dressing
3 c. dried fruit
6 sm. chocolate bars

Snack

Day 1

6 pitas
250g cream cheese
1 sm. red pepper

Day 2

1 bag corn chips
sm. jar salsa

Dinner

Day 1

Veggies & Dip
225g babaganoosh
4 carrots
4 celery stalks
1 small head broccoli

Main Course - Grilled Salmon
6 salmon fillets
6 cobs fresh corn
6 potatoes
salad dressing

Dessert
popcorn
2 chocolate bars
3 apples

Day 2

Garden Salad
1 pkg mixed greens
3 carrots
2 tomatoes
0.5 red pepper
250ml salad dressing

Main Course - Chicken Stir-fry
2.5 c. rice
6 chicken breasts
1.5 red pepper
1 sm. garlic bulb
1 red onion
9 mushrooms
1 head of broccoli

Dessert
200g blue cheese
200g old cheddar
1 pkg crackers
2 c. almonds
3 apples

SAMPLE MENU - 4 DAYS WITH 6 ADULTS

Day 3

Breakfast

6 oranges
3 c. granola
500ml yoghurt

Cinnamon Buns
6 c. Biscuit mix
.5 c. raisins
.5 c. brown sugar
cinnamon
.5 c. butter

Lunch

1 loaf rye bread
500g cheddar cheese
500g hummous
500g tabouleh
6 pears
6 granola bars

Snack

3 c. dried fruit and nuts
6 carrots
6 celery stalks

Dinner

2 pkg soup

Greek Salad
1 head of lettuce
2 tomatooes
1 cucumber
1 red pepper
can black olives
500g feta cheese
250ml greek dressing

Main Course - Dutch Oven Lasagna
1 pkg no boil lasagna noodles
14oz tomato sause
500g ricotta cheese
250g cottage cheese
500g mozarella cheese
1 onion
1 green pepper

Dessert - Dutch Oven Apple Crisp
8 apples
1 c. brown sugar
1 c. white flour
1/4 c. butter

Day 4

Breakfast

3 grapefruit
2 c. oatmeal
1 c. powdered milk

Pancakes
3 c. pancake mix
maple syrup
5 c. banana chips

Lunch

12 bagels
250g cream cheese
250g smoked salmon
sm. jar capers
1 sm. red onion
5 plums
1 pkg cookies

Snack

1 pkg rice crackers
250 g brie cheese
2 cans oysters

Dinner

2 pkg soup

Cabbage Salad
1 cabbage
2 carrots
.5 c. raisins
balsamic vinegar
olive oil

Main Course - Tuna Mac and Cheese
4 c. macaroni noodles
2 cans tuna
1 onion
2 carrots
1 head broccoli
250g cheddar cheese
1 c. powdered milk
.5 c. cheese powder

Dessert - Dutch Oven Chocolate Cake
1 pkg cake mike
powdered eggs
oil

Day 5

Breakfast

5 oranges
1 c. raisins

3 cooked potatoes
0.5 onion
1 can cooked ham
1 red pepper

Lunch

Logan Bread
500g cheese
1 cucumber
3 cans salmon
100 ml salad dressing
6 apples
6 granola bars

Snack

6 apples
3 c. gorp

Staples

4 lbs ground coffee
.5 lb coffee creamer
30 tea bags
spice kit
2 ltrs peanut butter
1 L honey
1 L jam
250ml mustard
3 lbs drink crystals
2 lbs hot chocolate
2 lbs powdered milk
3 lbs brown sugar
2 L cooking oil
1 lb margarine or butter
500 ml soya sauce

Other

1 bar charcoal briquets (for oven)
500 ml biodegradable dish soap
3 dish scrubbies
3 dish cloths
chlorine water treatment
matches and lighter

PACKING THE FOOD

The type of trip that you are planning will dictate how much consideration you put into your packing. For short trips, when space, weight and convenience aren't real issues, you might just pile your food into the food bag/barrel with the heaviest items at the bottom. For longer trips, you'll want to be more organized to save yourself time and frustration.

Once you've bought all your food, lay it out by meal from the beginning to the end of the trip. Measure out appropriate quantities and put each meal in separate, durable bags. Plastic freezer bags or reused milk bags closed with twist ties or elastics are economical and work well while zip-lock bags are convenient for staples (like tea bags) that will be opened many times. With your food broken down into days, it's helpful to write the contents on the bag in permanent marker, including the day it's for.

Here are some other tips for packing food:

- If there are several small items for one meal, bag them together so they are easy to find together.
- If there are directions that need to be followed (such as for cake or pancake mixes), tape the directions to the bag.
- Double or triple bag items that will make a big mess if they leak.
- If you don't want to transfer wetter foods that come in plastic containers, (like cottage cheese or yoghurt) into more dependably sealable containers (like Nalgene), put the containers in sealable bags, and/or put duct tape around the lids.
- Some fruits and vegetables pack and keep better if they are loose (like potatoes and oranges) but others (like tomatoes and grapes) are better stored in plastic bags to prevent them covering other food with juice and pulp if they spoil or are crushed. Keep close tabs on fresh fruit and vegetables because they tend to get wet with condensation. You may need to dry them off at times. If any fruit or vegetable shows signs of mould, get rid of it before it has a chance to spread.
- Glass jars can be packed if you're confident they won't get broken, but many parks prohibit the use of glass bottles, so you will need to transfer the contents to a plastic container.
- Carry "staple" items that you'll use on a daily basis together (such as coffee, tea, drink crystals, spices, etc.)
- Spices are best kept in small plastic containers.
- Tabasco and sauces in sturdy jars can be left in their original containers.
- Keep perishable foods in your fridge or freezer until the last possible moment before your trip so they'll keep longer.
- Meat can be frozen and wrapped in several layers of newspaper and plastic to help it keep a little longer.

When all the food is accounted for and labeled, you can start packing it. A 16 gallon (60 liter) barrel pack is the best way to keep the food in good condition. If you're using a pack with questionable waterproofing, you should double bag any food that must not get wet. Start with the last day at the bottom and keep the meals and days more or less in order. Pack crushable things away from cans and the edge of the barrel, and arrange the food as compactly as possible.

BREAKFAST

For many, neither breakfast—nor the day itself—begins until a coffee or tea has been had. Although instant coffee is a simple solution, there are a number of ways to make a fresh cup of coffee. You can use a French-press (Bodum), an old-school percolator, or coffee filters that require you to make one cup of coffee at a time. I prefer to use a tall coffee pot without the percolating apparatus, in which I'll boil water. Once boiled, I add fresh coffee grounds. After a minute or two, I'll swing the pot in big circles to settle the grounds at the bottom of the pot by centrifugal force. With coffee in hand, it's time for breakfast.

There are a number of ways to make a quick, easy and healthy breakfast. Some favorites include granola with yoghurt or milk (powdered, or fresh on short trips), and instant oatmeal. You can easily improve the meal with some small additions, such as nuts, raisins, fruit (dried or fresh), brown sugar, and cinnamon. Fruit is generally a great thing to include with every breakfast and there are some fruits that keep very well on trips. Oranges, apples and grapefruit will usually keep for over two weeks. Cantaloupe and melon carry well for up to three or four days. Canned fruit is another good option and will last longer than you! Dried fruit lasts a very long time, goes well in hot cereals, and can also be eaten on its own.

Mark swings the coffee pot in full circles to settle the grounds at the bottom.

Although these simple breakfasts can satisfy your appetite, they can be complemented with a second dish for variety or to provide an option for those who don't like cereals.

Pancakes are easy to make, especially if you bring a pancake mix that only needs water added to it. With some fresh fruit and syrup you'll be in heaven. Fresh eggs can be carried for a few days if they're kept cool, but it is a pain to keep them much longer than the first breakfast. Powdered eggs don't have the taste of fresh eggs, but they're virtually indistinguishable from fresh eggs in French toast, or when they're mixed with veggies and cheese in an omelet, breakfast burrito, or a quiche. For the meat lovers, vacuum-packed bacon will keep for a week or so. Dehydrated bacon tastes almost the same as fresh bacon and lasts for months. A hearty and warming breakfast for a cold day is fried potatoes with canned ham or bacon, vegetables and cheese.

If you have a little extra time and want to go that extra mile for your group, you should consider doing some breakfast baking. Muffin mixes and biscuits are quick to mix and take only 15 minutes to bake. Muffin batter can go in a single pan and be cut into wedges when it has finished baking. You can also make cinnamon buns with a simple biscuit mix. Using the bottom of your canoe and a Nalgene container, roll the dough out into a square or rectangle. Spread some butter on the dough and sprinkle it with raisins, nuts, brown sugar and cinnamon, then roll it into a long sausage and cut it into small slices. Lay the slices in a greased baking dish (they can be touching or not) and bake for 15 to 20 minutes at 350°F (160°C).

LUNCH

As well as refueling the engine, lunch is a time to recharge the mental batteries, do some exploring, relax and enjoy the surroundings. Although it is tempting to stop as soon as your tummy rumbles, try to choose a nice lunch spot with a good view, something interesting to explore and shelter if you have inclement weather. If you're not on a tight schedule, check your maps and don't be afraid to travel a bit out of your way to find an ideal stopping point. Even if you are trying to make good distance on that day, you'll travel more efficiently after a nutritious meal and a rejuvenating break. Before breaking camp in the morning, organize everything you'll need for lunch including the food, utensils, cutting boards, water filter, and the bathroom kit.

I usually just have a cold lunch but sometimes it is nice to have soup or hot drinks (especially if the day is damp or chilly) and these can be prepared quickly if your stove is easily accessible. Dishes can either be washed (if you've used lots of them) or just bagged and cleaned at supper. When everything is packed up, I like to pick a departure time that gives everyone enough time to filter water, relieve themselves, read, hike, and get psychologically prepared for the afternoon on the water. If you're catching and

eating fish, lunch is a great time to stop and cook it.

Lunch for me usually consists of some type of bread plus any of a variety of things to go inside or on top. When planning your breads, you need to consider how well they resist crushing and mould. Pitas and bagels travel well and will last four or five days in cool temperatures. Some rye loaves will last a week. Rich wholegrain loaves will last two weeks, but can be fragile. For the later part of your trip, choose dry and un-sliced loaves or bagels. Crackers and tortillas shells are a substitute for bread and will usually last a bit longer. On longer trips, making bread avoids the problem of bread getting crushed or spoiled. It's so tasty and easy that you may want to bake it on short trips too. Simple recipes like soda bread and Logan bread take 5 minutes to mix and then go straight into the oven for 45 minutes to bake. I prefer the Dutch oven for baking bread because it doesn't take up space on the firebox and you can pretty much ignore it while dinner is cooking. The challenge is to resist eating it as soon as it comes out of the oven, especially if the plan was to save it for the next day's lunch. If you have more time, yeast bread tastes great, and gets high marks for style. It takes about 5 minutes to mix and 5 minutes to knead but an extra 45 minutes to an hour to rise and knead again before it goes in the oven for baking. Any bread recipe will do, but I reduce the salt on cool days because it slows down the yeast.

To go inside or on top of your bread, peanut butter, honey and jam are convenient and nutritious staples. There is also a huge variety of cheese, salami, and dried meats that carry and last well. Canned meat, such as tuna and salmon are also popular and last forever. Dehydrated hummus and refried beans pack and keep well and can be easily re-hydrated for wraps or eaten as a dip. Lettuce and tomatoes are nice for the first few lunches, but will spoil very quickly. Celery, peppers and cucumbers last a little longer, but carrots, onions and pickles will last until the end. Don't forget to include mustards, relishes, hot sauces and other condiments in your shopping list as well, although you'll want to avoid real mayonnaise, which goes bad very quickly and easily. Sometimes in specialty food stores, you can find delicious and versatile spreads in small squeeze tubes that keep and travel well, like garlic, roasted pepper, or olive paste.

To top your lunch off, there's nothing like fresh fruit and treats like chocolate. There are many fruit options for the first few days, but when you're planning for the later stages of a trip, apples and oranges or dehydrated fruits are your best choice.

SNACKING

Even with a good lunch stop, you can expect stomachs to grumble in mid to late afternoon. Having some snacks on hand will go a long way towards keeping everyone happy and enthusiastic. Keep in mind that on trips, many people are more active

Snacks are an important part of any canoe trip and will go a long way towards keeping everyone happy and enthusiastic.

than in their normal lives and may find themselves enjoying sweets even if they don't usually eat them. Some favorite snacks include energy bars, granola bars, fresh fruit, nuts, chocolate, pepperoni sticks, hard candies and GORP (Good Old Raisins and Peanuts—though feel free to add all kinds of other stuff to the mix).

DINNER

Dinner is usually a relaxed social time, and you can expect that people will be ready for a hearty meal after a full day outdoors. Sometimes you might not have the energy or desire to cook anything but a simple meal, while at other times, the meal can represent the whole evening's entertainment.

However simple or complicated your dinner is to be, I've found that having hors d'oeuvres is always a great idea. It will temporarily fill the hunger gap, raise spirits, and even encourage people to help out with cooking the rest of dinner. Setting out the appetizers by the 'vegetable chopping station' is a sure-fire way to get results. Your appetizers can be as simple as a bag of nuts, carrot sticks, and cheese and crackers, or as classy as smoked salmon with capers, red onions and cream cheese on crackers.

Although a quick dehydrated dinner is sometimes the order of the day, I generally like to make dinner a three or four-course affair. I'll start with a soup, then a salad, a main course, and then finish with dessert.

SOUPS

Soups are great to take the edge off a hunger, and to cheer people up on a cold or long day. Soup mixes are compact and quick to prepare, making them ideal camp food. You might choose to skip this course on hot days but I pack them for each dinner. You can serve them as is, or add veggies such as onions, cabbage, beets, potatoes, or fresh herbs for variety.

SALADS

It is nice to have something fresh and crunchy every few nights. Lettuce will keep up to three or four days if it's cool, and cabbage will keep all summer. You can spice your salad up by adding some carrots, walnuts, raisins, cheese or other veggies. You can bring bottled salad dressings, prepackaged mixes, or you can bring oil, balsamic vinegar and spices separately to make dressing on your own.

MAIN COURSES

The options for main courses are endless. Some of the easiest and tastiest main courses include stir-fries, pasta dishes, fajitas, and fish. An oven opens up countless more meal options. Of course, for the first few nights you have the most options because you can use fresh produce and meat. Meat will last until the second night if it starts frozen and is wrapped in several layers of newspaper and plastic.

Rice appears on most trip menus because it goes well with most main courses, it packs well, and it cooks easily. As a general rule, you can budget 1/3 cup of dry rice per person for a meal. I like to use Basmati or long grain rice and here is my cooking method. Put a little more than twice as much cold water as rice in a pot and bring it to a boil. You can add spice or a touch of flavored oil at this point if you like. Do not stir the rice but continue to boil until the water is evaporated or absorbed and craters first appear in the rice. Cover with a tight lid and put on very low heat for 20 minutes—still no stirring. If you're cooking with a fire, you can set it beside the fire and take it on and off the coals occasionally to maintain the equivalent of a low heat setting.

Stir-Fries

Stir-fries in the wok are easy and leave lots of room for variation in ingredients and sauces. Onions will keep for weeks. Fresh red and green peppers, broccoli, cauliflower, zucchini, and mushrooms will last for up to five or six days in cool weather. All these vegetables are available dehydrated and still have a good taste and texture when they are re-hydrated and cooked. Carrots and many starchy root vegetables have the longest

Stir-fries are one of the easiest meals to make and leave lots of room for variation in ingredients.

lifespan and will last for a couple of weeks.

To make a stir-fry, start with a little oil and add the vegetables and meat according to cooking time. This makes a nice vegetarian meal, or you can add any sort of fresh, canned or dried meat. If you are going to add herbs, spices or sauces, add them early so the flavor can develop. Add cubed beef, potatoes, a beef broth cube and a bit of wine for a beef stew, or try throwing in some ham with maple syrup, Dijon mustard and pineapple. For a little more flavor still, you can add nuts near the end of the cooking or as a garnish. If you want to thicken the sauce, mix a couple of tablespoons of cornstarch or flour to cold water and add it to the stir-fry for the last 3 minutes of cooking. You can even turn your stir-fry into a fajita feast by using fajita seasoning for your sauce and then wrapping it all in tortilla shells with grated cheese and salsa.

Pasta

Pasta is another versatile favorite: macaroni and cheese, spaghetti, fettuccini, or even lasagna if you have an oven. Fresh pasta will keep 3-5 days and cooks more quickly, which is great if you need to conserve fuel. Otherwise, dry pasta works well. When cooking pasta, boil lots of water (at least 2 or 3 inches above the pasta, but the more the better), add some oil and then the pasta. Keep it boiling and stir it occasionally. While the pasta is cooking, dig a hole in the active layer of soil well away from camp and the shoreline (at least 50 feet, or 20 meters). When the pasta is ready, drain the water into the hole. This hole can also be used later for other "gray water", like toothpaste spit and dishwater.

You can either use pre-packaged sauces or make sauces from scratch. For a tomato sauce, cook some vegetables in the wok and add canned tomatoes, tomato sauce, or dried tomato sauce depending on the consistency of sauce you want. You can reduce the liquid and thicken the sauce by simmering it longer or by adding tomato paste. Basil and oregano go well in these sauces and parmesan cheese is a tasty garnish. To make a basic white sauce for four people, melt 2 tablespoons of butter over low heat, add 2 tablespoons of white flour, and then cook, stirring regularly for 3 to 5 minutes over low heat. Be attentive, because if it is not cooked long enough, the sauce will have a starchy taste, and if you cook it over too high a heat, it will burn and be bitter. Remove it from the heat and slowly stir in 1 cup of milk (which will likely be made from powdered milk) as well as any seasonings. Now return the sauce to the low heat and whisk it until it becomes thick and smooth. If you let it simmer a few minutes, it will be ready to serve almost right away, or you can add it to cooked veggies in the wok and let it simmer gently, so that the flavors can mix. If you opt for the latter, you'll have to stir the mixture regularly to prevent burning. You can then add cheese to the sauce just before serving.

Ruth and Jane put the sauce layer into the Dutch oven for a lasagna.

One of my family's favorites is cheese fondue. Heat a cup of white wine with a cup of milk, garlic nutmeg and pepper. It will curdle, but that's okay. Gradually add one and a half pounds of grated gruyere cheese and a half pound of emmental cheese. Mix 3 tablespoons of cornstarch with a quarter cup of wine and add it to thicken the fondue. You've now got a great dip for fresh, raw broccoli, cauliflower, onions, apple, cooked potatoes, cubes of cooked ham, and bread.

Baked Dinners

By bringing along some form of oven, you'll give yourself many more options for your meals. Dutch oven lasagna is one of my favorites, but you can also use it to cook things like stews, pot pies, deep-dish pizza, and quiche.

To make lasagna in a Dutch oven, start by making a tomato sauce with cooked veggies. Grease the oven and then put alternating layers of heated sauce, no-cook noodles (pre-soaked or dry), mozzarella, ricotta, and cottage cheese. The lasagna will take about 30 to 45 minutes to bake.

For a pot pie, start with a cream of mushroom soup in the Dutch oven. Add onions and other veggies, already browned or caramelized, or simply raw if you prefer. You can also add dried chicken or turkey, as well as spices like sage, basil and marjoram. Mix a couple of tablespoons of flour with a quarter cup of cold water and add that to the pot. The consistency can vary but you'll want the mixture to be thicker than soup before you begin baking. Once the mixture is ready, make biscuit dough and roll it out to be half an inch thick and the size of the Dutch oven. Lay the dough on top of the pot pie mixture and bake for about 40 minutes. The flour will thicken the mixture as it cooks.

DESSERT

After an active day in the outdoors, you can expect people to appreciate and have more room for desserts than they might in their normal lives.

Some of the best desserts are simple ones that offer campers something tasty to nibble on while hanging around the campfire. Try fresh fruits like apple, kiwi, and grapes along with cheeses, nuts, chocolate or cookies. A little port or ice wine is also a nice finish to a meal.

If you're prepared to cook a dessert, you might consider Rice Krispies squares. These are made easily by melting marshmallows and margarine in a frying pan and dumping in Rice Krispies. You'll also find several dessert mixes in the grocery store that don't require baking, such as cheesecake, mousse, or chocolate pie.

For a late night dessert or snack, you might want to try popcorn. You can make popcorn in the wok by heating three tablespoons of oil and a third of a cup of popcorn on a fairly hot fire. You'll need a large stainless steel bowl to use as a lid, and it's good to have some type of oven mitt. When the popcorn starts popping, keep the wok moving. When all the corn has popped, turn it upside down and serve it in the lid. You can even spice the popcorn up with things like butter, garlic powder, pepper, soy sauce, parmesan, or even cinnamon and brown sugar.

Apple crisp is a popular baked dessert that doesn't take too much work to make.

Baked Desserts

Most baked desserts take only 5 or 10 minutes to prepare, and about 30 minutes to bake with minimal attention while you eat the meal or relax around the fire. Just about any cake or brownie mix will work. Follow the directions on the box, substituting powdered eggs for fresh. Another favorite of mine is peach cobbler, which you can make with a can of sliced peaches, topped with white cake mix. Start with the peaches in the pan, and sprinkle the dry cake mix on top. Drizzle a half cup of melted butter and a half cup of coconut over top, and then bake it for 30 minutes. Apple crisp is also a popular dessert that doesn't take too much work—although making ice cream to accompany it presents a significant challenge.

On a trip on the Tatshenshini River in the far north, we tried making Baked Alaska to celebrate our crossing of the Alaskan border. By using ice from a nearby glacier with whipping cream and rock salt that we had brought, we made ice cream by hand. We then baked gingerbread cake and used thin strips of it to insulate the ice cream from the hot pan. On top of the ice cream went meringue that we whipped up from fresh egg whites. Although our impatience admittedly had an effect on the final result, it still tasted great.

OTHER FOOD CONSIDERATIONS

VEGETARIAN MEALS

For most meals, meat can be added after the vegetarians have filled their plates. If the carnivores in the group are open-minded, you can completely eliminate meat from the menu or use dried soy chunks or "texturized vegetable protein" (TVP) instead, which both taste better than they sound. They have a meat-like texture, are a good source of protein, and are a great meat substitute in stews, chili or stir-fries.

DEHYDRATED FOODS

Although there's no denying that fresh food tastes best, the simple fact is that it has a limited lifespan, and it can be bulky and easily crushed. Dried fruit and vegetables pack and keep very well and are great when cooked in sauces or stir-fries. Dried mushrooms, peppers, and broccoli re-hydrate very well, as does chicken and turkey. Dehydrated potatoes are also good for camping, because they are much lighter and less bulky to pack.

Although you can find more and more dehydrated foods in large grocery stores, outdoor stores now have an incredible variety of dehydrated meals. These meals often simply require the addition of boiling water and even come in packages that are designed to be used for the food preparation. Although I doubt you'll start eating these dehydrated meals at home, in the outdoors they seem to taste great and are incredibly convenient.

DISHWASHING

The best way to wash dishes in camp is to do so just like you would at home—with a hot water wash with soap, and then a separate hot water rinse. If you put a big pot of water on as soon as the meal comes off the fire or stove, you'll have dishwater ready when everyone is finished eating. You'll need something for scrubbing, a biodegradable soap, a flat surface (like the bottom of the canoe,) as well as two big clean pots. Although any pots will do, there are collapsible camp sinks made of coated material that work best for the job. You can then let the dishes air dry on the canoe before packing them away.

Before dropping your dishes into the wash pot, scrape off all the scrap food on to the fire or into the garbage. This will let your wash water go a lot further. When you're finished with the dishwater dump it in a small hole at least 50 feet (15 meters) from

The best way to wash dishes is with a hot water wash with soap, and then a separate hot water rinse.

shore and away from camp in the active layer of soil. If there is a lot of food debris in the water, pour it through a strainer and then throw the food bits into the fire or garbage.

It is important to understand that even biodegradable soap or food bits will have an effect on a sensitive aquatic ecosystem, not to mention detract from the next camper's experience, so do not wash your dishes in the lake or river. If you just have a few non-greasy dishes, you can wash them in a pot of cold water that will be dumped in the active layer of soil.

CHAPTER FIVE

SAFETY

CAPSIZE • SOLO TRIPPING • PROTECTION FROM THE ELEMENTS
LEADERSHIP • BEARS • WEATHER

Canoe camping safety begins in the planning stages of a trip. Remember that the trip that you choose needs to fall within the comfort zone of everyone in your group, because your group is only as strong as the weakest or least experienced member.

The biggest hazards when deciding on whether or not your group is ready for a particular route is your exposure to wind, waves, cold water, or long crossings. These adverse conditions can be safe and a lot of fun for more experienced paddlers with proper gear, but can be dangerous for less experienced or poorly equipped groups. As a general rule, the larger the body of water is, the more susceptible it will be to strong winds and waves. Wind and waves will make it difficult to turn or steer and can potentially swamp or capsize a canoe, depending on their severity and your paddling skills. If you're planning to go to a region with cold water, you'll need to be even more conservative with your trip plans because hypothermia is a serious concern in the event of a capsize.

Once you've picked an appropriate trip and are on the water, know that common sense, a conservative attitude, a clear-eyed acknowledgement of potential hazards and a little preparation are all you need to pull off a safe and enjoyable canoe camping experience in accessible and protected areas. For example, you don't have to be a weather expert to detect threatening clouds approaching, nor do you need to be a doctor to notice yourself or others becoming hungry, cold, or tired. Appropriate actions should be taken before these small concerns become dangerous situations. As conditions change, you need to continually ask yourself, "is there a real risk that if someone in our group capsized right now, they could not be easily rescued and avoid hypothermia?" The key to staying safe is in making the decision to get off the water before the answer to that question would be "yes". This often means that someone in your group needs to take leadership in the moment and make it happen.

CAPSIZE

Capsizing on a flat-water canoe trip is rare and not a major concern, as long as you're in calm conditions, close to shore, your gear is waterproofed, and you're wearing appropriate clothing for the water temperature. Most flat-water capsizes happen while getting in and out of the canoe, so you're often in shallow water where you can stand up. If you venture further from shore than is reasonable to pull your boat and gear into shore, or plan on making a long crossing, it becomes very important to learn a canoe-over-canoe rescue.

CANOE-OVER-CANOE RESCUE

The canoe-over-canoe rescue is a technique that allows an upright canoe to empty a capsized canoe and get the swimmers back in their canoe. When a canoe capsizes, your first concern should be for the paddlers in the water. The best place for them is at the ends of your boat, where they can grab hold of your boat without destabilizing it, and wait for you to empty and right their canoe.

In the rescue canoe, the first thing to do is to pull up to one end of the overturned canoe. Your bow paddler will then focus on stabilizing your canoe while the stern person grabs one end of the capsized canoe and then pulls it over the gunwale until it is centered and out of the water. The stern paddler will then flip the canoe upright and slide it back into the water. As long as the packs were tied into the canoe on a

After a capsize, the rescue boat should pull up perpendicular to the upside down canoe and the swimmers should go to the ends of the rescue boat.

The stern paddler pulls the upside down canoe across their boat while the bow paddler stabilizes the rescue boat.

The stern paddler flips the empty canoe upright and slides it back into the water.

The paddlers in the rescue boat hold the empty canoe while the swimmers reenter from the side.

15 to 20 foot (5 meter) rope, they will float beside the canoe and not hamper this operation. The swimmers can then make their way around to the far side of the now-empty canoe, where they can climb in one-at-a-time while you stabilize their canoe by holding and putting weight on the opposite gunwale. While you continue to stabilize their canoe, the paddlers can retrieve their packs and bail out any remaining water.

SOLO TRIPPING

Canoe tripping solo or with one other person can be very rewarding, but I would not recommend it to anyone who is inexperienced in camping and paddling. Without a partner or another canoe, you'll simply have fewer options available if a rescue or emergency situation arises. Issues that would be inconvenient for a group can become major concerns or even life-threatening for a single person or canoe.

PROTECTION FROM THE ELEMENTS

HYPOTHERMIA

Hypothermia is a lowering of the body's core temperature and is a real hazard of outdoor living—even in summer. The key to avoiding hypothermia is not letting yourself get cold in the first place. This might sound simple—and it is—but is important to understand that it is much harder to warm up than to just stay warm. If you start to get a chill, take the time to put on another layer. Make sure that you keep your body energized by drinking lots of water and eating high energy foods. Dressing appropriately makes a huge difference because the speed at which you lose body heat increases when you are wet, exposed to wind, and when in contact with something cold (water or ground). Proper clothing includes adequate insulation, wind protection and water protection. It's important that you wear quick-drying and wicking materials against the body. Remember that cotton is one of the all time worst materials to wear against the body because wet cotton will actually conduct heat away from your body.

HYPERTHERMIA

Hyperthermia, (also known as overheating, heat stroke, or heat exhaustion), is an easier problem to deal with than hypothermia, but it can sneak up on you and quickly spiral out of control. It is caused by a dangerous rise in the temperature of your body's core which, left unchecked, requires medical treatment. Fortunately, it is easily avoided

when canoe camping because water is an ideal cooling system. The first line of defense is protecting yourself from the sun by wearing a hat, sunscreen, and staying in the shade whenever possible. If you find yourself starting to overheat, go for a swim, have a drink, and get out of the sun.

LEADERSHIP

Group dynamics are different on every trip. Many canoe trips proceed quite well without a leader. Deciding how much spice to put in the chili or when to get up in the morning will be more efficient with an autocratic leader, but can be more entertaining in an anarchy or democracy. On a family trip, Mom or Dad might assume this role, or the kids can take turns being leader for the day (under the watchful eye of the parents). On commercial trips, the hired guides are the appointed leaders. Private groups often have a natural leader who perhaps has more experience, or was simply the one who sent the invitations and bought the maps. Other groups will have no established leader and will share the tasks and decision-making. This can work well for small groups, but as groups get larger it becomes more important that there is an acknowledged leader. This leader can assume a fairly passive role and let the group self-govern for the most part, but step in to gently diffuse conflicts within a group, or to provide effective direction and group coordination in emergency situations.

More often than not, bears will run away at the slightest indication of human presence. The most dangerous bears are surprised bears, or ones that feel you to be a threat to themselves or to their young.

BEARS

One of the reasons we go on canoe trips is to see wildlife, but some of these encounters are unwelcome. Remember that we are visiting animals' homes and there is usually a reason for their behavior.

For many, there is great comfort in knowing that wild Black and Brown bears, even Grizzlies, are naturally and typically more afraid of us than we are of them. More often than not, bears will run away at the slightest indication of human presence—and they can usually smell and hear us from quite far away. The most dangerous bears are surprised bears, or ones that feel you to be a threat to themselves or to their young, and their responses are not predictable. Do not get between a mother and her cubs. If you see a cub, you can be certain that the mother is nearby and you should vacate the premises as quickly as possible without drawing attention to yourself. If you are walking in dense bush where you suspect there might be bears, make some noise to alert them of your presence—singing, occasional clapping or banging, and exuberant conversation work well. In a face-to-face encounter, bears may become curious and move downwind of you, or stand on their hind legs to assess you. You should stand together as a group, make a bit of noise, and have bear spray or a rock ready to throw if they get too close. Let them check you out because they will usually move along when they decide you aren't a threat. Running away may encourage an attack, but moving slowly away is fine. A lone, small bear may be discouraged with rocks or sharp noises, but be very cautious about how aggressively you behave, in case they decide to take up the challenge.

Bear spray is an effective deterrent for bears that are not being scared off by the usual methods. Bear spray is a pressurized canister of pepper spray that has a range of about 15 to 20 feet (4 to 6 meters), but be very careful that you are upwind of the bear before using it. Cracker flares or "bear bangers" produce sharp noises that can also scare a problem bear away.

If a bear has learned to not fear people and that humans can be a source of food, its behavior can be unpredictable. They may even enter occupied campsites in search of food. You can help prevent this situation and improve your safety by keeping the campsite clean, dumping your gray water far from camp, and keeping the food inaccessible. At the end of the day, make sure all the food is packed up and that you don't have any food or scented things in your tent at night. Barrel packs are the best protection for food against bears. I will usually leave the barrels in the kitchen area clamped shut but if I have food in a dry bag that leaks odors more easily, and is more easily chewed or carried away, I will hang it in a tree away from the tents and out of reach of bears. For more information, see the section about "Closing Camp for the Night" in Chapter 3.

WEATHER

An interesting part of canoe tripping is watching weather systems develop and change. Most weather you will experience on a trip shouldn't affect your plans as long as you are well-equipped. In fact, I love paddling in a teaming rainstorm. Still, there are some conditions in which you shouldn't be on the water.

WIND

Strong winds can make it difficult to steer your canoe, create hazardous waves on large bodies of water, and often make paddling not worthwhile for the amount of headway you'll make relative to the effort required. In many cases, you're best off hanging out in camp and waiting for a strong wind to die down before getting on the water.

A storm rolls in during a canoe trip down the George River in Northern Quebec.

LIGHTNING

Thunder and lightning storms are spectacular from a safe distance, but nerve racking when experienced up-close. Knowing that sound takes about 5 seconds to travel a mile, (3 seconds to travel a kilometer), you can get a good idea of how close lightning is by noting the time between the lightning bolt and the thunder clap. Lightning can also occur half a mile (about a kilometer) from the edge of a storm, and it likes to strike the tallest object—which is you when you're on the water—so get off the water at the earliest indication of lightning.

Lightning will strike hilltops, tall objects, or exposed ground and can travel through tree roots, water or swampy ground. The best place to take shelter is amongst low trees, and not directly under tall trees. For further protection, you can insulate yourself from the ground by sitting on a pack or your PFD. If you are in the middle of a lightning storm, it's not a bad idea to separate the group into smaller groups. On the extremely odd chance that someone is struck, others will be safe and able to help.

CHAPTER SIX

ACTIVITIES

**THE SOCIAL SCENE • FISHING • PHOTOGRAPHY • GAMES
CAMPING WITH KIDS • CAMPING WITH DOGS • WHITEWATER**

THE SOCIAL SCENE

While it is nice to have a lake to yourself it is rare that other canoeists or campers detract from your experience and the fact that others are there enjoying the area is going to help ensure that our recreational resources remain protected. Some of my best memories from years of guiding on the Nahanni River are from meeting people from other groups, comparing experiences and having fun together. Like many routes, the Nahanni has an abundance of great campsites, so if someone is camped where you were planning to stay, you'll usually find an equally spectacular spot just around the bend. In areas where campsites are few and far between, you may have to share a campsite to avoid a group having miserable camping spot or an arduous extension to their day's travel. Be a gracious host or thoughtful guest and make the best of the situation. You may have a grand time and meet some new friends.

When the paddling day is over, wine or cocktails can complement an evening but there are a few considerations. First of all, glass bottles are heavier, and require more care than decanting liquids to a Lexan container. In addition, glass and even alcohol are prohibited in some parks. More importantly, consume alcohol responsibly. You may not be driving a vehicle, but unexpected situations might arise where you'll need all of your wits about you, such as a bear encounter or a first aid issue. It's also important that you be considerate of other groups in the area and keep your noise to a respectful level.

FISHING

For many people fishing is the reason for a canoe trip and it will often get you to some rarely fished waters. Just make sure you carry appropriate licenses for wherever you're fishing and check for local information about locations, species, lures and flies. You could fill a canoe with the fishing gear that some anglers use but you can also travel light. For the ultimate in compactness, there are some good and simple collapsible rods available.

There are many opportunities for fishing on a trip. Fish are often more active in the morning and evening but if your rod is handy, you can take a few casts at lunch or any time you're stopped. You can trawl a line while you're paddling but your normal paddling speed is faster than an effective trawling speed and if you get a snag, you'll hold up the rest of the group getting it off. You may want to be a bit sensitive to the pacing of the trip for benefit of the non-fishers in your group. However, if it is part of the objectives, you may want to fish when you see fish or good conditions. On the first

day of a trip on the Chuluut River in Mongolia, we saw several huge taimen that had the fishermen in the group drooling. We passed up the chance to cast our lines with the thought that we'd be able to do so when we got to camp. That night the water rose and turned muddy so we didn't get good fishing conditions for the rest of the trip.

Some people prefer to catch and release but fresh fish is an excellent supplement to your menu. If there are bears in your area, remember that they like fish too so clean your hands after handling fish and if you are cleaning fish, don't do it close to your campsite. Use a rock or piece of wood at the shoreline and throw the rock in the water or burn the wood afterwards. The entrails and head can go back in the water, deep enough that other campers won't see the remains.

PHOTOGRAPHY

Any canoe trip deserves to be captured on film, whether you think of your images as snapshots or creative art. The unfortunate truth is that although many cameras are taken along on canoe trips, a remarkable number of them never make it out of the case. The reason is usually as simple as the camera not being easily accessible. By making your camera easily accessible, your photography will be more fun and less intrusive on the others in your group. You'll also get better wildlife photos and candid people shots. In order to keep your camera easily accessible, you'll want some type of case that protects it from bumps and water. The best cases are hard, waterproof cases that a company named Pelican is renowned for. You can also use soft waterproof cases, such as those by AquaPac and Watershed, although they won't protect your camera from being knocked around as well as the Pelican case will. If you want to have the flexibility to shoot in wet or rainy conditions, the best option is a point-and-shoot waterproof camera. Another option is to use the AquaPac waterproof camera case, which has a clear lens through which photos can be taken while the camera stays completely dry.

Another big reason that cameras aren't pulled out of their cases is that it can be difficult and awkward to do so without holding up the whole group. If you expect to get any good photography done, you need to plan ahead. You may need to paddle ahead so that you can climb up on shore and get your shot without falling behind the rest of your group. It will also make a big difference if you pack up your gear and load your canoe quickly in the morning so that while others are still getting ready, you are free to capture the moments.

Mark plays a portable guitar—a great instrument to bring along on camping trips.

GAMES

Games are often missing from our busy lives and a trip is a perfect time to enjoy these simple pleasures. There are many games that are perfect for a canoe trip. I often take a Frisbee for any big gravel or sand bars that we might come across. A hacky sack is nice to have handy and to get the legs moving when you're off the water. Skipping stones is a pastime that can be elevated to an art form. One of my favorites is the rope pull. With two people standing on rocks or stumps about a meter apart, you each hold onto a single piece of rope that is 10 to 15 feet (2 to 3 meters) long. The goal is to pull all of the rope from the other person without falling off your rock.

CAMPING WITH KIDS

A canoe trip is a wonderful time to spend with your family and can be a great experience for children of all ages. A ride in the canoe for our first newborn was the only thing other than the vacuum cleaner and a bumpy ride in the stroller that would stop his crying. In fact, he still cries when he doesn't get to go canoeing. Kids—just like adults—must always wear PFDs when canoeing. Be aware that an adult-sized PFD will not be suitable for children. Lifejackets need to fit properly in order to be

Canoe camping is a great experience for kids. Just remember that kids get bored fast if their curiosity and creativity aren't engaged.

effective, and there are many kid-sized PFDs on the market at very affordable prices. Kids also need a paddle, although you may want to tie the paddle to the canoe so that it doesn't get lost.

Of course, paddling with kids has the potential of being a trial for everyone involved, but here are a few tips to help make it a happy experience. Have a comfortable space for them in the canoe where they can reach the water. The younger the child is, the more sensitive they'll be to sun, dehydration and hunger. With small children, don't plan to go far. Their needs must dictate your schedule. With older kids, set manageable and rewarding goals and don't smother them with rules or technical paddling advice—let them try it their way. Don't expect kids to enjoy spending extended periods of time quietly sitting in a canoe, or efficiently paddling in rhythm for hours. If your plan is to complete an ambitious three-hour tour of the entire lake shoreline (with minimal pit stops), then a full-on mutiny should also be on your schedule. Kids get bored fast if their curiosity and creativity aren't engaged, so wherever possible let them set the goals and make up the games. Their imaginations will astound you, and in seconds, they'll be using a canoe in ways that you never even considered. If you do "need" to cover a certain amount of ground, bribery is always a valid option. Bring small treats along for the ride and you'll be able to keep kids interested and happy for a bit longer.

Around camp, all of the little tasks, such as putting up the tent, collecting wood and cooking, can be fun if kids are involved. Come to think of it, this applies to adults as well—almost anything can be fun if you let it be. Although it's not a bad idea to bring toys or some other form of distraction, the most interesting things may well be dragging a hand in the water, a lily pad, a frog, a chipmunk, or a stick in the fire. Teach them, learn from them, and enjoy.

CAMPING WITH DOGS

In some parks and camping areas, dogs are not allowed. They can be a nuisance to other campers, to local wildlife, and they tend to leave very odorous signs of their passing. If dogs are allowed where you're going, this doesn't mean it's a good idea to bring yours. Some dogs can be ideal traveling companions while others would be happier at home—where they should stay. Vocal dogs are also bad candidates for canoe camping because they will negatively affect the experience of other canoe campers in your area and frighten wildlife.

In a canoe, most dogs have good balance, although they'll want to see what is going on and when they feel unstable, they'll be more comfortable standing up. They need to learn that you decide when they should get in and out of the canoe, notwithstanding the duck that just took off in front of the canoe. Something else to consider is that if your dog is used to being inside at home, they'll want to be inside at night. If you think they'll be happy in the tent's vestibule while you're in the tent, think again. Bugs can be just as annoying to animals as people. They also may need a little help understanding the tent screen, which can be quite amusing. At times, you may want to have them leashed on the campsite to prevent excessive exploring or encounters with the local wildlife.

WHITEWATER

Unfortunately, many people believe that whitewater canoeing is only for the hardcore adventure seekers, willing to challenge Mother Nature head on. The reality is that whitewater paddling can be as relaxing and enjoyable, or as challenging and heart-pounding as you want it to be. As long as you have a slightly adventurous side and the willingness to get your head wet, then you're a real candidate for whitewater canoeing. By learning to paddle safely and comfortably in whitewater, you'll dramatically increase your options for canoe trips, you'll develop a set of skills and confidence that allows for canoe tripping in more challenging weather and water conditions, and you'll gain access to some of the most spectacular parts of the country.

Learning to paddle a canoe in whitewater, you'll dramatically increase your options for canoe trips and gain access to some of the most spectacular parts of the country.

If you're interested in learning to navigate a canoe through whitewater, the only good option is to take a course from a reputable whitewater paddling school. You'll learn how to read whitewater, recognize hazards, and all the strokes, skills and rescue techniques that will make your time on the water as safe as possible. You'll also learn how to use safety and rescue equipment that aren't necessary to have on regular canoe trips.

GLOSSARY OF TERMS

Barrel pack A 8 or 16 gallon (30 or 60 liter) waterproof plastic barrel for carrying gear

Bear spray A pressurized canister of pepper spray that is an effective bear deterrent

Bow The front of a boat

Canoe-over-canoe rescue A deep water assisted rescue in which the capsized canoe is emptied of water and the paddlers returned to the canoe

Capsize The flipping of a canoe from right-side-up, to upside-down

Compass A magnetic device that indicates direction relating to magnetic north

Dry bag A waterproof bag for equipment

Dutch oven A cast iron or aluminum pot that is used for outdoor baking

Firebox A collapsible metal box used to contain a fire

GPS (Global Positioning Unit) A battery-powered electronic device that very accurately calculates positions and courses based on satellite information

Gunwales *(pronounced "gunnels")* The structural aluminum, vinyl or wooden rails along the top of the canoe hull

Heading The compass direction of travel to a destination

Hull The bottom of the canoe

Hypothermia A dangerous condition caused by a lowering in the temperature of the body's core

Hyperthermia A dangerous condition caused by a rise in the temperature of the body's core

Navigation The art and skill of determining your position, and selecting a safe route to your intended destination

PFD Personal Flotation Device or "Life jacket"

Paddle Canoe paddles are single-bladed devices for propelling the boat; kayak paddles have two blades

Portage (noun) a trail linking two navigable waterways; or (verb) the act of carrying a canoe and equipment between two waterways

Put-in The location where you start your trip

Satellite phone A phone that receives and sends its signal via satellites

Staples Menu items that get used at most meals

Stern The back of a boat

Shuttle The process of getting a vehicle from the put-in to the take-out of a trip

Take-out The location where your finish your trip

Thwart A wooden bar across the canoe that keeps the boat stiff

Topographical maps Maps that include contour lines showing the height of the land above sea level

Wannigan A plastic or wooden box for carrying kitchen equipment

Water filter A hand held pump with a ceramic or fiberglass filter to remove viruses, pathogenic bacteria and protozoa from untreated water

Water treatment Methods of treating fresh water to kill viruses, pathogenic bacteria and protozoa and render the water safe to drink

Whitewater Current or moving water in a river

Wok A bowl-shaped, steel cooking pan

Yoke The centre bar in a canoe that is sculpted to rest on your shoulders when carrying the canoe

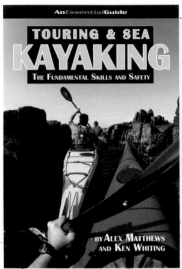
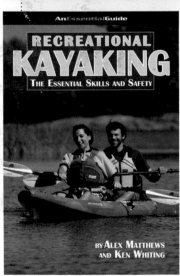